COMMUNITY DEVELOPMENT AS A PROCESS

COMMUNITY
DEVELOPMENT
AS A PROCESS

LEE J. CARY, Editor

University of Missouri Press
Columbia

ISBN 0–8262–0097–4
Library of Congress Card Number 74–130699
University of Missouri Press, Columbia, Missouri 65201
Printed and bound in the United States of America
Copyright © 1970 by The Curators of the University of Missouri

PREFACE

Books usually are the products of individual authors or of two or three colleagues in collaboration. Books of readings often include the previously published works of many, united through a common framework by the volume's editor. This book, the work of seven authors, is not a reader. The contributing authors wrote each chapter specifically for this volume. The editor recognized the need for a basic volume on community development as a process, drew up a tentative outline, and then set about to involve those in the field who seemed best qualified to contribute.

The results—the involvement of six colleagues who, together with the editor, contribute information beyond what any one author could accomplish. Although the chapters vary somewhat in style, together they offer a complete commentary. The book has a unity beyond that which one might expect from seven men working independently of one another.

Part One discusses the concept of community development and the context in which the process takes place. Irwin T. Sanders, author of the first chapter, is well known for his book *The Community: Introduction to a Social System*. His many contributions include "Theories of Community Development" in the March, 1958, issue of *Rural Sociology* and his chapter on "Community Development Programs in Sociological Perspective" in the book, *Our Changing Rural Society: Perspectives and Trends*. The second chapter, written by Roland L. Warren, focuses on the context of community development. Warren's books, *The Community in America* and *Perspectives on the American Community*, and recent articles growing out of research and teaching at The Florence Heller Graduate School for Advanced Studies in Social Welfare at Brandeis University, made him a most logical choice to discuss the context of community development.

Part Two consists of three chapters devoted to the community development process itself and to the sociological and psychological implications of the process. Willis A. Sutton, Jr., of the University of Kentucky, presents the sociological implications of the community development process. His article, written with Jiri Kolaja on "The Concept of Community," in the June, 1960, issue of *Rural Sociology*, and "Elements of Community Action," in the May, 1960, issue of *Social Forces*, demonstrate his interest and understanding in this area. Warren C. Haggstrom discusses the psychological implications of the community development process in Chapter 4. The impact of the process upon people and their lives is a major research interest of Warren Haggstrom and is reflected in his own organizing efforts in Syracuse, New York, and on the West Coast. Dan Schler, a former fellow faculty member at the University of Missouri–Columbia, has introduced a number of students to the field through his course on the theory and principles of community development. His discussion of community development process, in Chapter 5, gives some indication of the comprehensive introduction these students have received.

The third and final part of the book is concerned with the roles of the citizen and the community developer. I undertook to examine the community's participation in the process, since this is a central interest in both my teaching and my research. Robert Morris discusses the role of the community development agent in Chapter 7. He has written widely on community planning and is author, co-author, and editor of several volumes on the subject.

This book addresses several audiences. While it is suitable for use in certain upper divisional and graduate courses in sociology, social work, and related fields, it is specifically intended for students in community development at both the undergraduate and graduate levels. In addition, the book should find an audience among the growing number of workers and citizens involved in community development, community organization, and community action programs both here and abroad.

I wish to thank the other six authors who have contributed their work to this book and also my colleagues in the Department of Regional and Community Affairs for suggestions and helpful comments. I hope that this book will contribute to the professional preparation of a whole new generation of community developers and to their understanding of community development as a process.

L. J. C.

Columbia, Missouri
June, 1970

CONTENTS

INTRODUCTION

The organization of people in a locality to deal themselves with problems and opportunities close at hand that affect their lives and patterns of living is the central theme of community development. Since World War II there has been increasing emphasis on community planning and action that involves the citizens' participation. This kind of planning calls for citizens to engage in the setting and implementation of goals that they will themselves carry forward to fruition. Throughout the world, the successful transition from colony to independent country rests, in part, on the ability of the new governments to involve their people in the process of building a nation. In the United States a major emphasis of most recent national, state, and area programs is on the citizen and on his involvement at the local level, where action, because it touches his life, can be most effective.

Community development, as Irwin Sanders points out in Chapter 1, can be viewed as a process, a method, a program, or a movement. The major thrust of this book is to emphasize community development as a process. This emphasis agrees with much of the literature in the field and if thoroughly understood should lead to the further development and refinement of practice in this relatively new profession. Beyond emphasis on process is alertness to the intangible effects on people, brought about through this process. "The emphasis," again referring to Sanders, "is upon what happens to people psychologically and in their social relationships." The approach is an orderly manner of proceeding to improve the community through the united efforts of the people in carrying out their own plans and programs.

A number of definitions of community development are available.[1] Essentially, community development is "the delib-

1. See Peter du Sautoy, *The Organization of a Community Development Programme*, 121–30; William W. Biddle and Loureide J. Biddle, *The Community Development Process: The Rediscovery of Local Initiative*, 78; Roland L. Warren, *The Community in America*, 324; also Irwin T.

erate attempt by community people to work together to guide the future of their communities, and the development of a corresponding set of techniques for assisting community people in such a process."[2] While no widely accepted definition is available to the reader, a few important elements or aspects of community development appear again and again in the literature. These elements together provide a generally acceptable definition of the process; they are: (1) community as the unit of action; (2) community initiative and leadership as resources; (3) use of both internal and external resources; (4) inclusive participation; (5) an organized, comprehensive approach that attempts to involve the entire community; and (6) democratic, rational, task accomplishment.

Community, as the term is used here, refers to people who live in some spatial relationship to one another and who share interests and values. The community may be an urban neighborhood, town, city, county, region, or any other combination of resources and population that makes up a viable unit. In fact, the community may be any grouping of people with shared interests who live within a delimited area. Sutton stresses the importance of what is "collective for" rather than what is "local to" a population, recognizing that geography is operationally important rather than substantively distinctive. The unit of action, the arena for the process, is the community as we have defined it here. While much of the people's activity may go on within a part of the community or beyond it, the community remains the focus for their lives, and it is the unit to which the community developer addresses himself.

A second important element in community development is *local initiative and leadership*. The direction for the process is derived internally, not externally. People from within the community must assume the leadership positions. If they are not prepared to do so, then leadership training becomes an item with high priority for the community development staff. As Ross points out, "development of a specific project (such as an

Sanders, "Theories of Community Development," *Rural Sociology*, 23, No. 1 (March, 1958), 4–5.
2. Warren, 20.

industry or school) is less important than development of the capacity of a people to establish that project."[3]

The *use of resources from both within and outside* the community is another aspect of community development. The "great change" mentioned by Roland Warren in Chapter 2 and discussed in detail in his book on *The Community in America,*[4] refers, in part, to the increasing number of decisions concerning the community that are being made external to the community. Concurrent with this phenomenon is the fact that many of the resources needed by the community lie outside its jurisdiction. Therefore, to carry out program and to bring about change, the community not only draws on its own strengths and capabilities but it also looks beyond for various forms of assistance. The problem in practice becomes one of knowing what resources are available where, and how to work with the community so that it achieves the most effective blend of its own resources with those from outside. Ohlin refers to this effective use of internal and external resources as "a more flexible fit of the rule systems of major social institutions to the distinctive life styles of the local community."[5]

Inclusive participation, a fourth important element, does not mean that all members of a community participate in all community undertakings or even that a large percentage play some role. Inclusive participation means that all segments and groups within the community are given an opportunity to take part. Further, special efforts may be necessary to assist certain groups to organize as the first step toward active participation. Whatever organizational structure emerges should be "open-ended" to the extent that new groups, as they become identified and organized, can become a part of the ongoing process. This element suggests that such organizations might have a somewhat fluid membership, based on the particular activities at any given time and on the degree of interest of various segments of the community in such activities.

3. Murray G. Ross, with B. W. Lappin, *Community Organization: Theory, Principles, and Practice,* 15.
4. Warren, Chap. 3.
5. Lloyd E. Ohlin, "Indigenous Social Movements," in *Social Welfare Institutions,* Mayer N. Zald, ed., 181.

The term *organized, comprehensive approach* is the companion concept to *inclusive participation*. While rational community decision-making can focus on only a limited number of the issues and concerns faced by a community, those selected should come from the broadest spectrum of situations and should call upon the widest range of resources. A truly comprehensive approach is an ideal that will not be found in the real community but, as an ideal, should serve as a goal for which the community strives. Too many community efforts are already too narrowly conceived, too segmented in approach, and too closely oriented to the interests of limited groups within the community. Community efforts, to reflect that term fully, require broad participation in a comprehensive approach to specific goals. This broad participation means intensive and extensive involvement throughout the community, plus the investment of substantial resources toward the carrying out of specific community decisions.

The process by which these specific community decisions are put into action must be democratic, rational, and oriented toward accomplishment of the specific task. The organization that undertakes this process carries a responsibility that goes unrecognized by many people. Bloomberg points out "there are *no* major formal organizations in the community which have as a central function the cultivation of citizenship. No institutional sector is devoted primarily to motivating participation in community affairs, developing the needed skills among the citizenry, and facilitating and organizing their involvement and participation in the recognition, definition, and resolution of community problems and issues." Bloomberg goes on to say, "With the exceptions of elections and referenda, our ideology of local democracy would therefore seem to depend for its implementation more upon an informal and always emergent organization of community members than upon the formally organized institutional sectors."[6]

This book does not present a "domestic" and "foreign" view of community development. The process is seen as having general application as a means of group decision-making and

6. Warner Bloomberg, Jr., "Community Organization," in *Social Problems: A Modern Approach*, Howard S. Becker, ed., 374.

community change in a variety of settings—traditional, transitional, and urban-industrial. To be sure, each situation has certain differentiating characteristics, but the process, allowing for these differences, is generally applicable. Warren points out in Chapter 2 that as a method for bringing about social change, community development is being used at the present time in situations which are predominately rural and preindustrial and in situations which are urban and industrialized: It is being used as a means both of promoting industrialization and a means of coping with its consequences. This latter distinction is of greater importance in the application of the process than the more apparent distinctions between the foreign and domestic settings.

Community development can be viewed as both a radical and a conservative process. It is radical to the extent that, in calling for greater citizen participation, it creates new groupings and patterns of decision makers. It tends to challenge existing social systems. It accelerates the pace of planned change and deliberate community decision-making. It broadens the scope of citizen interest and concern. All these factors tend to suggest new activity, new patterns of involvement, and change that is more rapid and involves more people more directly than at any time in history. Compared with previous community decision-making, it can indeed be viewed as a radical process.

Community development can also be seen as a conservative process. It helps to keep decision-making at the local level and government responsive to the local citizens. Community interest is apt to center on issues close at hand. Even among the decisions that are made at a higher level of government there is some opportunity for local option and variations. This is "grass roots" democracy, with the local citizens recognizing, defining, and resolving their own problems and issues. However, this book does not address itself to the political implications of the process. Such matters are so important that they should be treated in a separate volume.

As I remarked in the Preface, this book is divided into three parts. Part One deals with the concept of community development and the context within which the process takes place. Part

Two considers the sociological and psychological implications of the process, followed by a chapter that develops an overview of the process orientation in community development. Part Three focuses on the two major participants in the process— the citizen and the professional. The book is directed to people in the community who are interested in understanding more about this process of community development. While of particular interest to the student in community development, community organization, or related fields, these chapters should prove as valuable to the interested citizen and participant in the process. The book was not conceived as or written to be an introductory text, yet a person can read it as a first book in community development. It should prove of greatest value as a reference book and as a book of collateral reading, since it gives greater emphasis to the community development process than is found in much of the literature.

PART ONE   The Concept and
Context of Community Development

Before we discuss community development as a process and the implications of the process, we need first to consider what community development is all about and to identify some of the earlier efforts out of which it has evolved. We need also to look at the arena in which the process takes place: the setting for action. Irwin Sanders and Roland Warren, in Chapters 1 and 2, establish this background and framework in their discussion of the concept and context of community development.

Sanders begins the book by reviewing some of the earlier approaches to social betterment, with community development growing out of a union of *community* organization—stressing local action and local resources, and economic *development* —emphasizing planning and systematic movement toward defined goals. Community development also owes much of its earlier evolution to rural sociology, adult education, and the extension movement. It is recognized that community development is not the only developmental approach to social betterment and that economic, agricultural, industrial, and social development are other efforts directed at changing social conditions.

Sanders discusses four ways of viewing community development: as a *process*, a *method*, a *program*, or a *movement*. As the terms are defined by Sanders, this book's emphasis is on community development as a process, and the seven authors stress this orientation throughout. The concept of community development that one gains from this first chapter is that of an emerging social process which has not yet established its identity as a separate profession. Borrowing from many disciplines, it has begun to develop its own theory expressed in terms of basic elements or principles to be applied for effective practice.

The context in which community development occurs, the subject of Chapter 2, is the local community. But there are at

7

least two major contextual considerations beyond the local community that greatly affect the process—whether the activity is part of a regional or national plan or distinctly local and whether the community is located within a predominantly rural, preindustrial setting or an urban, industrial complex. Warren refers to these as the *less developed* and the *more developed* context. In the rural or less developed context the community development process tends to help bring about industrialization and modernization. In the more developed context the process may be a means to help cope with the effects of industrialization and modernization.

Warren's concept of "the great change" includes a number of great sweeping changes occurring in most parts of the world (increase in population, people moving to the cities, the spread of urban ways) as well as the decline of the locality as the central focus of association. As Warren points out, the context within which community development occurs is significantly different according to the extent to which the particular country or region has experienced various aspects of *the great change*. While the process is essentially the same, regardless of setting, in the urban complex, community development is apt to be carried out through one of two forms. It operates at such a "superorganization" level that it fails to engage most people in any meaningful way; or it focuses on an extremely narrow slice of the total community picture in terms of limited issues or limited geography, such as a neighborhood.

One of the major dilemmas in the field is noted by Warren when he indicates that at the same time that community development is increasingly being employed as a process to help influence the course of change at the community level, an increasing number of community affairs are influenced by events and decisions that occur beyond the community. The reciprocal interrelationship of local community concerns and the affairs and conditions of the region and the nation, therefore, becomes increasingly important. The problems of these relationships and some suggestions for working them out forms the final portion of Chapter 2.

CHAPTER 1

The Concept of Community Development

IRWIN T. SANDERS

Community development is new as a discipline, but its lineage is honorable and well established. Its newness is shown by the fact that in 1948 the United Nations Organization assigned one community development adviser to one country; in 1966 approximately 61 such experts were working in 29 countries. Its ancestry may be viewed as a union of *community* organization and economic *development*. The older *community* organization concept is itself a mixture of Utopian socialism and the strong accent on local action. In Western Europe this concept led to welfare programs administered through local governments; in the United States it resulted in the organization of community welfare councils and other efforts at community improvement, which were private more often than government programs. Recently, however, public funds—federal, state, and local—have flowed in increasing amounts to programs dealing with social problems in American cities.

The economic *development* side of the heritage of community development introduced the idea of process, of stages through which economies and societies had to pass in order to reach desired goals. Thus, the linkage of community organization, which stresses local action and use of local resources, with economic development, which emphasizes national planning, careful allocation of resources, and systematic movement toward defined goals, could have come about only at a particular juncture in time—which happened to be in the post-World-War-II era. The importance of this timing becomes clearer as one learns more about these forerunners of community development.

Man's history is dotted by innumerable efforts to improve communal life. When conditions in one place became intolerable and promised little improvement, those who dreamed of a better life might move off to set up a new community more to

9

their liking. Among those who remained, some leaders might try to bring about local action to deal with pressing problems. In some instances, their efforts succeeded. Thus, the new discipline *community development* does not describe a new, untried human experience but gives a particular shape, suited to modern times, to the long-standing human urge to act collectively to improve the group's lot.

EARLIER APPROACHES TO SOCIAL BETTERMENT

THE UTOPIANS. We need look only to our own history to find many examples of individuals who banded together to form a new community in which they hoped to put into effect some religious or economic principles not generally prevalent in the larger society. The Shakers, an English offshoot of the Quakers in the first half of the eighteenth century, founded new communities in the United States, the chief one being at Mount Lebanon, New York. Some of their principles were unique. There was no marriage. When married couples joined the society they treated each other as brothers and sisters, and the two sexes occupied rooms in separate parts of the houses. There was careful division of labor, the men doing the farming, gardening, and industrial tasks; the women, the housework, including tailoring and repairing the members' garments and preparing seeds, herbal medicines, butter, and cheese for sale. Everybody worked. The community paid due respect to civil law but refused military service during the Civil War, which coincided with their heyday. Sheltered in these communities, the members were free to practice their religious ceremonies and to deny themselves the use of alcohol (except for medicinal purposes), tobacco, and flesh-meat or fish. Inevitably, since these communities were dependent upon adult recruits primarily and not upon biological replenishment, they eventually died out.

A second highly publicized community was set up at New Harmony, Indiana, on the Wabash River, in 1825 by Robert Owen and his son Robert Dale Owen. The land (38,000 acres) was acquired from the Harmonists, who had settled there in 1815 in an effort to found an ideal community. The Owens invited "the industrious and well disposed of all nations" to join with them in a community where all goods were held in common but regulated in use according to age and where religious services were to be replaced by "moral lectures." Unfortunately, the Owenites included many who were not industrious, in contrast to the Shakers, and so the community was an economic failure after a short period. But this effort caused much discussion in Europe and America as to what community life should be.

Another well-known Utopian community was Brook Farm, founded in 1841 near West Roxbury, Massachusetts. It excited interest because of the fame of some of its supporters, among whom were Nathaniel Hawthorne, Ralph Waldo Emerson, and Margaret Fuller. This community, formed into an association, stressed the principles of cooperation. Everyone shared equally in the work, the pay, too, being equal for all kinds of work. All shared equally in educational advantages and in social enjoyments. Much attention was paid to the school, where even college subjects were part of the curriculum. In 1847 a devastating fire destroyed most of the property. With this economic loss, enthusiasm for the project waned and the association dissolved.

A final example to be mentioned is the Oneida Community, established in 1847 in Madison County, New York, by what were then known as Communists or Perfectionists. After a slow start, the community became financially successful because of the development of numerous industries. The community had a complex marriage system in which couples were not formally married and recognized no permanent ties. Children born of these unions were the responsibility of the whole community. The Oneida domestic system aroused opposition by neighboring communities, so, in 1881, the free marriage system was abolished and the community was reorganized as a joint-stock company. Community of property was also discontinued, but the principle of cooperation was retained in economic matters.

Today in the United States some so-called "intentional communities" exist, constituted by those who wish to adhere to some economic or social principle the community represents.

In India and elsewhere efforts are being made to form settlements where brotherhood and other values are incorporated into the daily life of the inhabitants.

These illustrations of community life would not today be classed as community development. They are important historically in that they show how people have tried at various times to reach certain goals by modifying community life from that which was prevalent about them; they also show the difficulty of keeping at a viable level any community organized in a greatly different pattern from those in the surrounding society.

ORGANIZED CHARITIES. Even before the turn of this century one of the chief approaches to community problems in the United States was the charity organization society. Its forerunners were relief societies, which sought to coordinate almsgiving among the poor and in some cases to change the living conditions of the less fortunate. A feature of the charity organization society was its city plan, which incorporated all of the ways in which the leaders sought to control the social environment of the growing cities. The plan called for support by local municipal revenues and for the careful investigation of the needs of clients. Investigation of needs and allocation of funds and services, in turn, led to the demand for more and better trained social workers; in response, schools for the training of social workers were founded. Part of the city plan of the charity organization society was the cooperation among churches and societies, with the former providing spiritual counseling and, when deemed necessary, assistance in the reformation of the needy, the society providing the material relief. Such societies in the United States were confined chiefly to the largest urban centers—150 or more—the smaller places following the more traditional, informal methods of assisting their dependent and delinquent citizens through local churches and county government.

This approach to social problems was based on the clear recognition that those who were fortunate had a special responsibility to those who required help. It also represented a systematic, coordinated approach that led toward professionalization of those who devoted full time to providing this help. The society attended to problems that already existed, but it was unsuccessful in carrying out plans, such as those put into effect in the New Deal under Franklin D. Roosevelt in the 1930's, to prevent the social problems that resulted from a rapidly changing society.

COMMUNITY ORGANIZATION. World War I brought with it the need to mobilize communities to support the war effort—to sell Liberty Bonds, provide morale-building materials for the troops at the front, and in some cases take care of servicemen's families. Thus, the social scientists and social workers of that period had firsthand experience in community organization, which transcends the charity organization societies already mentioned. E. C. Lindeman, in his book *The Community*, published in 1921, set forth for the first time ten steps in community action.

The conditions on the home front during World War II necessitated even more sophisticated patterns of community organization. By the late 1940's, therefore, many social workers had come to realize that part of the welfare worker's task was the management and counseling of such groups as the community chests, welfare councils, and various social planning groups. As a result, instead of concentrating solely upon *case work* (which deals with individuals and families as clients) or upon *group work* (which deals with individuals in groups), specialized training became available also in *community organization* (the total set of structures dealing with welfare and recreation in a community).

Paralleling this evolution in the welfare field, sociologists continued their examination of American communities. They used the term *community organization* to mean the total structure of the community (religious, governmental, economic, educational, etc.) and not merely organization for social welfare. This dual use of the term persists, but causes little difficulty if one takes the trouble to note the context within which it is used. Indeed, many people still prefer to use *community organization* to describe programs designed to improve community life in the more developed countries and reserve *commu-*

nity development for such efforts in the developing countries. Nevertheless, the latter term is given increasingly wider use in the West.

DEVELOPMENTAL APPROACHES TO SOCIAL BETTERMENT

ECONOMIC DEVELOPMENT. Economists were the first to deal systematically with the development of communities on any appreciable scale. They saw the great contrast between the economies in sub-Saharan Africa, for instance, and those in Western Europe or the United States. They asked how the one could develop toward the level of the other. How does one accumulate capital, in a country in which most of the people merely subsist, sufficient to support a satisfactory banking system, insurance and pension arrangements, investment in industry and transportation, and funds for farmers to use in modernizing agriculture? The flow of public and private resources from richer to poorer countries and the efforts of less developed countries to raise domestic savings through reinvestment of growth income have contributed to capital accumulation to make modernization possible.

The programs that have aimed at consciously bringing about economic growth have often dealt primarily with either the agricultural sector or the industrial sector. Obviously, any overall economic plan would include both sectors, but specific economic programs in which rapid change is expected must focus on particular targets.

Agricultural development, which at first glance would seem to deal in simple fashion with increasing agricultural productivity, is a highly complex cluster of activities. One of the clearest descriptions of this process is that by Arthur T. Mosher in his *Getting Agriculture Moving*.[1] Not only does Mosher discuss the compelling necessity to produce more food and fiber for a rapidly growing world population, but he also indicates the importance of increased agricultural production for the

1. Arthur T. Mosher, *Getting Agriculture Moving: Essentials For Development and Modernization*, Agricultural Development Council (New York: Frederick A. Praeger, 1966).

industrialization of the country. Furthermore, he relates agricultural development to human development as follows:

> For agricultural development to occur, the knowledge and skill of farmers must keep increasing and changing. As farmers adopt more and more new methods, their ideas change. They develop a new and different attitude toward agriculture, toward the natural world that surrounds them, and toward themselves. . . . Their increasing contacts and transactions with merchants and government agencies draw them into closer acquaintance with the world beyond their villages. They increasingly become *citizens*, full members of the nation. . . . Agricultural development thus is an integral part of general social and economic development. It contributes to it, and it assures that over-all development shall be truly general, including within its scope the large proportion of people who live by farming—and who will for many years continue to live by farming in many countries.[2]

Industrial development is the conscious effort to promote industrialization or "the extensive use of inanimate sources of power for economic production, and all that that entails by way of organization, transportation, communication, and so on."[3] According to Wilbert E. Moore, those engaged in industrial development must make certain that four types of conditions are met in addition to the more obvious economic matters of capital formation, determination of investment ratios in the various sectors of the economy, or the character of foreign assistance and foreign trade. The first set of conditions lies in the realm of *values*:

> The value of economic growth requires, for example, a fairly high degree of individual mobility and a placement system grounded on merit in performance, and that requirement is likely to come into conflict with a number of strongly supported values relating to the primacy of kinship position and obligations as a moral virtue. In this sense extensive value changes are the most fundamental condition for economic transformation.[4]

2. Mosher, 11–12.
3. Wilbert E. Moore, *Social Change* (Englewood Cliffs, N. J.: Prentice-Hall, Inc., 1963), 91–92.
4. Moore, 92.

Moore also points out that rapid modernization is frequently associated with the value of nationalism.

A second set of conditions is *institutional*. In the case of labor, it must be mobile both geographically for relocation and socially for motivation and prestige. A third economic institution—a system of exchange—must be commercialized so that the more efficient monetary terms are the bases for wages and prices as well as for business transaction. In addition, rationality must be institutionalized to the point that some leading sectors of the population are not only committed to the ideal of economic growth but also use rational means toward achieving that ideal.

Industrial development is also dependent upon two other sets of conditions: *organization* and *motivation*. Some administrative organization or bureaucracy must come into existence to link the technology of the factory with the techniques of specialization and coordination. Other aspects of organization are the fiscal apparatus of the state to equip it to serve both as banker and tax collector, "social overhead capital" in the form of transportation and communication, and local "housekeeping" for the provision of housing, streets, water, and other public services.

Motivation, as expressed in ambition for personal betterment and the acquisition of education and skills to further that ambition, must exist in some groups initially and then spread to other groups if economic development is to occur. In conclusion, Moore points out that a widespread sense of participation in changing the social order is a more helpful condition for economic growth than mere passive adjustment by the majority of the population to the drive and direction of a minority.[5]

The necessity for economic planners to decide what proportion of available funds are to be distributed to the agricultural sector, what part to the industrial sector, what part to education and to "social overhead capital" confronts them with difficult choices. The more they know about the nature of economic development, the wiser will be their allocation of these

5. Moore, 93–97.

resources and the better will be their evaluation of the effectiveness with which they are being used.

SOCIAL DEVELOPMENT. The description of these facets of economic development shows how closely it is related to many social factors. Some programs of change select special factors for emphasis and try to move them ahead of others in a developmental sense.

One big problem related to modernization in the developing countries and to betterment of life in the urban slums of the industrialized countries is the effective literacy of the population. Easy comprehension of the printed page is indispensable for modern living. Shortly after its establishment, the United Nations Educational, Scientific and Cultural Organization (UNESCO) began a massive program of Basic Education, through which it sought to teach people to read and write and thereby lead them to significant changes in their personal living as well as in their communities. Education is one recognizable aspect of personal and social development. More recently, with the establishment of the Center for Educational Planning as an affiliate of UNESCO, increased emphasis has been given to educational improvement at the national level. Through studies, publications, and conferences, this center tries to teach educational planners in the emerging nations the various sequences to follow in building strong educational systems and the priorities to establish among the goals they set for themselves.

As for development in the social welfare field, Ellen Winston, United States Commissioner for Welfare, has mentioned two current views of social welfare. One view places it in a residual role, in that it comes into play only when the normal structures of society break down. A second view "defines welfare activities as a front line function of modern industrial society, in a positive, collaborative role with other major social institutions working toward a better society."[6] The American society has demonstrated once and for all that economic changes

6. U.S. Department of Health, Education and Welfare, *Social Development: Key to the Great Society*, Welfare Administration Publication No. 15 (Washington, D. C.: 1966), 1.

bring social dislocations that require the attention of social welfare workers. The developmental approach would necessitate economists' and welfare specialists' working together to anticipate social consequences of planned economic programs. They would devise programs to assist families that might otherwise break up; to the health, educational, and physical needs of children; to self-fulfillment by adults as they pursue recreational and leisure-time pursuits; and for social security through provisions for unemployment, retirement, and illness.

Elizabeth Wickenden has related social welfare to development as follows:

> Thus "social welfare" . . . includes those pioneering, adaptive, and ameliorative services through which a society seeks to insure to its population the answer to those particular social needs which are considered essential to its own functioning but which are not adequately met by other instrumentalities including the family. It is both compensatory (in the sense of picking up where others leave off) and innovative (in the sense of showing the path toward a better total social adaptation). Its role in development operates not only on the latter side but also in the services it renders which make individuals, groups, and communities better able to adapt to the changes implicit in the developmental process.[7]

This brief discussion of economic and social development highlights their interdependency and describes significant efforts directed at changing the human condition. Where, one might reasonably ask, does community development fit into this spectrum? That is what this book is all about. To begin our search for an answer we might start out with the kinds of meaning given to *community development*.

WAYS OF VIEWING COMMUNITY DEVELOPMENT

One way to cut through the variety of meanings given to *community development*, whether by the different professions,

7. U.S. Department of Health, Education and Welfare, *Social Welfare in a Changing World: The Place of Social Welfare in the Process of Development*, Welfare Administration Publication No. 8 (Washington, D. C.: 1965), 27–28.

social scientists, or national leaders, is to note four ways that those involved seem to view it: as a *process*, a *method*, a *program*, or a *movement*.[8]

COMMUNITY DEVELOPMENT AS A PROCESS. In this view community development moves by stages from one condition or state to the next; it involves a progression of changes in terms of specified criteria. It is, in this view, a neutral, scientific term, subject to fairly precise definition and measurement expressed chiefly in social relations: change from a state where one or two people or a small elite within or without the local community make decisions for the rest of the people to a state where people *themselves* make these decisions about matters of common concern; change from a state of minimum to one of maximum cooperation; change from a state where few participate to one where many participate; change from a state where all resources and specialists come from outside to one where local people devise methods for maximal use of their own resources. The emphasis here is upon what happens to *people* psychologically and in their social relationships. A few representative definitions illustrate this view:

> A process of social action in which the people of a community organize themselves for planning and action; define their common and individual needs and problems; make group and individual plans to meet their needs and solve their problems; execute these plans with a maximum reliance upon community resources; and supplement these resources when necessary with services and materials from governmental and non-governmental agencies outside the community. (United States International Cooperation Administration.)[9]

J. D. Mezirow sees the community development process as

> a planned and organized effort to assist individuals to acquire attitudes, skills, and concepts required for their democratic participation in the effective solution of as wide as possible a

8. For fuller statement, see Irwin T. Sanders, "Theories of Community Development," *Rural Sociology*, 23 (March, 1958), 1–12.

9. United States Government, International Cooperation Administration, *Community Development Guidelines*, Airgram Circular, October 27, 1956 (Washington, D. C.: 1956).

range of community problems in an order of priority determined by their increasing levels of competence.[10]

Richard W. Poston defines community development as

an organized educational process which deals comprehensively with the community in its entirety, and with all of the various functions of community life as integrated parts of the whole. Thus the ultimate goal of community development is to help evolve through a process of organized study, planning, and action, a physical and social environment that is best suited to the maximum growth, development and happiness of human beings as individuals and as productive members of their society.[11]

Lowry Nelson, Charles E. Ramsey, and Coolie Verner see community development as an "education-for-action process." The process helps people achieve group goals democratically; the leader becomes an agent for constructing learning experience rather than the proponent of a program for community improvement; primary importance is attached to the individual. Furthermore, it is problem-oriented at the community level; the means employed in the solution are more important than the solution itself; and it is one of several types of purposive change.[12]

A United Nations definition gives the national government major importance:

The process by which the efforts of the people themselves are united with those of governmental authorities to improve the economic, social and cultural conditions of communities, to integrate these communities into the life of the nation, and to enable them to contribute fully to national progress.[13]

10. J. D. Mezirow, "Community Development as an Educational Process," *International Review of Community Development*, No. 5 (1960), 137–38.

11. Richard W. Poston, Report of the Chairman, Division of Community Development, Annual meeting of National University Extension Association, Salt Lake City, Utah, 1958.

12. Lowry Nelson, Charles E. Ramsey, and Coolie Verner, *Community Structure and Change*, 30–31, 417–19.

13. United Nations, Administrative Committee on Coordination, "Twentieth Report of the Administrative Committee on Coordination to the Economic and Social Council," Annex III. Document E/2931 of 18 October 1956.

Curtis H. Mial, in defining community development as a democratic social process whereby citizens participate fully in improving their own environment, notes that the process puts the emphasis on "the manner of proceeding."

> This implies that it is possible to follow an orderly progression from exploration and initiation through study and discussion to action and evaluation. It puts the emphasis, too, on the local group, on local initiative, on local participation. Finally, it puts the emphasis on full responsible participation and action by all the people affected.[14]

Frank H. Sehnert, after analyzing many definitions of community development, decides to view it "as a process for changing communities toward desired goals. Included in this process are study, training, education, planning, organizing, and action that brings about the cognitive purposeful change toward the community goals."[15]

COMMUNITY DEVELOPMENT AS A METHOD. Some view community development as a means to an end, a way of working so that some goal is attained. Other methods (such as change by degree or fiat; by use of differential rewards; by formal education) may be supplementary to the community development method, which seeks to carry through the stages suggested under *process* in order that the will of those using this method (national government, private welfare agency, or local people themselves) may be carried out. The process is guided for a particular purpose, which may prove "harmful" or "helpful" to the local community, depending upon the goal in view and the criteria of the one passing judgment. The emphasis is upon some *end*. Central planners, economic developers, and those representing some one professional field may look upon community development in terms of whether it will or will not help them achieve the concrete, material goals they have in mind. In the literature, of course, the terms *process* and *method*

14. Curtis H. Mial, "Community Development—A Democratic Social Process," *Adult Leadership*, 6, No. 10 (1958), 277–82.

15. Frank H. Sehnert, "A Functional Framework for the Action Process in Community Development," (Carbondale: Department of Community Development, Southern Illinois University, 1961. Mimeographed).

are often used interchangeably. For instance, Nelson, Ramsey, and Verner, who were quoted earlier as viewing community development as a process, also state that it "has come into being in recent years as one of the most significant techniques for the application of research findings to the resolution of major problems." In this sense, it may be conceived as a function of government and be established as a department or bureau appropriately designated; it may be the methods utilized in effecting certain forms of social organization (community development *for* social welfare, *for* recreation, or *for* public health); it may be confused with community organization, which refers to the study of *existing* patterns of community structure and interrelationships; or it may disguise *techniques for manipulation*.[16]

While still considering community development as a process, Howard McCluskey thinks of it also in terms of *method*, as "the induction and educational management of that kind of interaction between the community and its people which leads to the improvement of both." It is "a method of teaching adults the use of timing and the sequence of activities in bringing a project through successive stages to an acceptable closure."[17]

Of course, many community practitioners who actually regard community development as a process, when they are urging its benefits with government officials and others who have not yet been won over, argue its merits as a method of economic as well as social development.

COMMUNITY DEVELOPMENT AS A PROGRAM. When one adds to the method, which is a set of procedures, some content—such as a list of activities—one moves toward a community development program. By carrying out the procedures, the activities are supposedly accomplished. When the program is highly formalized, as in many five-year plans, the focus sometimes tends to be upon the program rather than upon what is happening to the people involved in the program. It is as a program

16. Nelson and others, *Community Structure.*
17. Howard McCluskey, "Community Development," in *Handbook of Adult Education in the United States*, Malcolm S. Knowles, ed. (Chicago: Association of the U. S. A., 1960), 416–20.

that community development comes into contact with subject-matter specialties such as health, welfare, agriculture, industry, recreation, and the like. The emphasis is upon accomplishing sets of activities, which can be quantified and reported.

Arthur Dunham, who views community development as "organized efforts to improve the conditions of community life, and the capacity for community integration and self-direction," identifies four basic elements in such efforts: (1) a planned program; (2) encouragement of self-help; (3) technical assistance, which may include personnel, equipment, and supplies; (4) integration of various specialties for the help of the community.[18]

Isabel Kelly indicates the personnel problem in community development when viewed as a program:

> Today in many nations, the development of village-level programs approximates epidemic proportions. Sometimes these are called community development, but the principles and procedures usually associated with the latter appear likewise in programs focussed on agriculture, health, nutrition, education or something else. The overall technical and administrative aspects may be admirable and financial support so generous as to constitute a sizable slice of the national budget. Nevertheless, the really critical point is that of contact with the community, and here success generally rests largely on the performance of the village-level worker who, as a rule, has scant preparation for such heavy responsibility.[19]

Even those who stress community development as a process or a method soon find themselves involved in a program. In fact, most efforts go into getting a program started and, once under way, to keeping it going. T. R. Batten, who considers the field of community development to include any action taken by any agency and primarily designed to benefit the community, does deal essentially with programs. He observes that one of the principal problems in using democratic methods in community development is that the central govern-

18. Arthur Dunham, "The Outlook for Community Development: An International Symposium," *International Review of Community Development*, 5 (1960), 33–55.

19. Isabel Kelly, "Suggestions for the Training of Village-Level Workers," *Human Organization*, 21, No. 4 (1962–1963), 241.

ments put pressure on village-level workers to achieve national goals within given time periods. As a result, the village workers attempt to speed up the programs with less democratic methods.[20]

A United Nations definition puts the emphasis on program most clearly. The term *community development*

> designates the utilization under one single programme of approaches and techniques which rely upon local communities as units of action and which attempt to combine outside assistance with organized local self-determination and effort, and which correspondingly seek to stimulate local initiative and leadership as the primary instrument of change. . . . In agricultural countries in the economically underdeveloped areas, major emphasis is placed upon those *activities* which aim at promoting the improvement of the basic living conditions of the community, including the satisfaction of some of its nonmaterial needs.[21]

COMMUNITY DEVELOPMENT AS A MOVEMENT. For some, community development becomes a crusade, a cause to which they become deeply committed. It is not neutral, like process, but carries an emotional charge. It is dedicated to *progress* as a philosophical and not a scientific concept, since progress must be viewed with reference to values and goals that differ under different political and social systems. Community development as a movement tends to become institutionalized, building up its own organizational structure, accepted procedures, and professional practitioners. It stresses and promotes the *idea* of community development as interpreted by its devotees and has its charismatic leaders who can enunciate its ideology in forthright terms.

As early as 1948 the Cambridge Conference on African Administration characterized community development as

20. T. R. Batten, *Communities and Their Development*, 2; *Training for Community Development*, 6–7.

21. United Nations, International Labor Organization, Committee on International Organizations, Program of Concerted Practical Action in the Social Field of the United Nations and Specialized Agencies, Document E/CN 5/291, 1953.

a movement designed to promote better living for the whole community with the active participation, and if possible on the initiative of the community, but if this initiative is not forthcoming spontaneously, by the use of techniques for arousing and stimulating it in order to secure its active and enthusiastic response to the movement. It embraces all forms of betterment.[22]

In 1957, however, a conference held at Hartwell House, Aylesbury, England, spoke of community development as an idea rather than as a movement, with its own content, its own skills, and its own officers.

Peter du Sautoy, experienced in community development in Ghana, defines it as a "philosophy as well as a process," thus emphasizing its idealistic as well as its practical aspects. To him, an important feature of a community development program is its organization, used as a source of stimulation but not as a source of domination.[23]

Robert Janes, in assessing community development in the United States, sees two forces threatening it as a movement and as a major guide and agent in the field of community action: the growth of the influence of the profession of city planning, and the direct intervention of the federal government in the process of initiating local action programs. As defenses Janes proposes the increased professionalization of the agents of the community development tradition and better public relations through which they explain the tradition to a broader public. This professionally trained personnel must have clearly defined roles in community action that can be identified along with those to be played by city planners, social welfare workers, and others.[24]

22. *Community Development*, Handbook prepared by a Study Conference on Community Development held at Hartwell House, Aylesbury, Buckinghamshire, September, 1957 (London: Her Majesty's Stationery Office, 1958).

23. Peter du Sautoy, *Community Development in Ghana*.

24. R. W. Janes, "Measure of Effective Community Development: An Appraisal of Community Action as a Social Movement," *International Review of Community Development*, 8 (1961), 5–13.

TYPES OF PROGRAMS. Community development programs vary in many respects. Some have a limited geographic range, such as slum areas of cities (ACCION in Venezuela, the Delhi Pilot Project in India) or a few villages (Save the Children Federation in Greece); others are regional, such as the Tennessee Valley and Upper Michigan projects in the United States, the Eastern Forestland of the Netherlands, or Sardinia; others are national, such as the comprehensive governmental plans of India, Ethiopia, and Venezuela or the programs of national organizations such as the U.S. General Federation of Women's Clubs. Some programs make use of volunteers, whereas others rely almost exclusively upon a trained professional staff to activate the local population toward community improvement. Some programs are comprehensive in that they are trying to move ahead on a broad front, integrating many scattered ameliorative attempts, whereas others tend to select one or two themes, such as illiteracy, for major stress. Experience has shown, however, that the general programs need increasingly to use specialists and that the programs organized around a single purpose need to broaden their scope. Programs differ, too, in the extent to which local people participate in program planning and in contribution of money, labor, and materials. Programs may seek to motivate cooperation through the citizens' self-study of their community and its problems, intercommunity competitions for awards, tangible material benefits (such as subsistence wages), or appeals to nationalistic pride and sentiments. Typically, some local group advises the community development personnel and serves as a clearinghouse and as a channel of communication. In some programs, professional personnel do not go into a community unless invited by local leaders, whereas in others a village-level worker may live in a village for a while before broaching the full details of the community development program.

In general, those most interested in community development as a *process* work with a much less detailed program, permitting each community to move ahead with its own felt needs, which may differ from those of other villages in the country; those who view community development as a *method* tend to work with a program that has been drawn up at a central headquarters and that specifies the goals each village is expected to achieve in agriculture, health, or education; those who stress the *movement* introduce an evangelistic fervor that gives the program a momentum that might otherwise be lacking.

In national programs, administrative problems arise concerning the relationship of the community development apparatus (whether as a separate ministry or a bureau or division of the ministry) to the old-line ministries of agriculture, transportation, welfare, economic coordination, and the like. Officials from these ministries who are "seconded" or loaned to the community development program realize that the advancement of their careers lies with their home ministries and not with community development. But to set up a completely new community development staff without making use of such specialists means uneconomic use of the trained manpower pool. The strain between the program's needs for specialists and the specialists' ambitions explains why community development programs receive less favored treatment from government officials except in those instances when the chief of state makes clear his strong support of the program.

THE PROFESSIONS' VIEWS OF COMMUNITY DEVELOPMENT.   There is a tendency for some professions to try to capture a dominant role in any field as new and popular as community development. The field of education made the first start by seeking to identify community development with adult education or with basic and fundamental education. Some aspects of adult education do go beyond instruction in formal courses to programs of local action, and these can be viewed as part of the educational process.

Agricultural extension specialists, especially in the United States, have seen in rural community development programs a chance to apply the techniques of social organization and communication that have helped raise American agriculture to its present high level. At times, extension workers have viewed community development programs as a threat to their programs or as an unnecessary addition, demonstrating a preference for their traditionally much narrower approaches over the comprehensive community development plans.

More recently, social workers, as they extend their views to international programs, see in community development an excellent vehicle for the expanded expression of Western social work philosophy and organizational methods. Some would equate community development with community social welfare organization, particularly in urban settings. In Great Britain, sociologists and social anthropologists, because of their concern with the processes and techniques of social change, see community development as an applied field of their disciplines. Their contributions lie in setting forth general strategy and the formulation of a program designed to achieve specified community development goals. On the whole, economists have clearly distinguished between economic development and community development, with most of them showing little enthusiasm for the latter. Political scientists, while recognizing that community development may in an emerging nation be one form of helping rural people to identify with a central government, have tended to focus more on public administration than on community development, which loses its essence if too rigidly administered. Politicians, on the other hand, gauge community development by its effect upon their own and their party's power.

A particular program in a given country may be under the sway of a single professional group, but community development, as it evolves as a world-wide phenomenon, is apt to draw from all related professions and in turn contribute to their enrichment. Indeed, some practitioners suggest that community development become a profession, correlative with social work, for example. The University of Missouri grants a graduate degree in community development, and numerous universities in both the Central States and Canada have departments or bureaus of community development that perform teaching and service functions. There are also training institutes for community development workers in several countries, one of the most notable of these being at Comilla, in East Pakistan. Community development is, however, still too young a field to justify any long-range predictions about its identity as a separate profession or its combination with any other.

Principles and Theory

Like any emerging profession, community development has begun to develop its applied theory, set forth chiefly in the form of principles of action, which should be followed for effective practice. Each mature practitioner, since community development is so new, has perforce come from some other discipline or profession. His background shows in the lists of principles he sets down or passes on to his associates. Some stress the psychological overtones of motivation and group dynamics; others, the sociological caveats of recognizing social values and social structure; others, the administrative aspects of sound programming; and still others, the anthropological investment in cultural change, the educators' concern with learning, or the specialists' concern with appropriate technology.

Lacking at the present time is a body of tested theory on developmental change and the connection between community development and other types of development. Nor do we know in any systematic way why some programs succeed by the developers' standards and other programs fail. To date—and this is a crucial test—existing training programs do not draw upon any identifiable community development theory as such, but rely almost entirely upon social science generalizations that have been developed quite apart from community development activities.

An excellent example of the use of social science principles is found in work done by Frank and Ruth Young. They have carried out cross-cultural studies on how communities grow, quite apart from consciously planned programs of community development. What kinds of local institutions come into being first, as people try to meet the requirements of modernization? They present five generalizations:

1. *Communities develop according to a cumulative, unidimensional sequence.* The development is cumulative in the sense that the presence of any given step in growth implies the presence of all of the "lower" items. Moreover, deviations from the sequence are so few that one can conclude that only one

dimension is being tapped—namely, an underlying developmental process.

2. *The sequence holds for communities of all sizes and in all cultures.* Cross-cultural items tend to be broad and abstract. One would look for a full-time religious specialist, not for a Protestant minister.

3. *Internal institutional growth is identical with external elaboration of communications.* Institutional differentiation thus has two sides: one that faces in and the other that faces outside the community. A public plaza not only serves the needs of local people but it has an external aspect in that it is the point to which most visitors from outside are most likely to go upon arrival in the community.

4. *Direction of community growth is always toward greater participation in the national social structure.* Local institutions become increasingly articulated with their national counterparts.

5. *Population size of the community increases in direct proportion to the degree of articulation.*[25]

The Youngs make clear the implication of their type of analysis of community growth to community development:

> Up to now we have conceived of community development as the voluntary efforts of residents under the guidance of an outside leader. . . . Success or failure has been unpredictable and explanation of results has been embedded in the context of the events in particular villages. The development theory outlined here contrasts with this view by calling attention to the importance of the level of community articulation at the beginning of the experiment and the sequence through which the community must pass. While voluntary efforts may speed progress or widen the scope of influence of a community within given levels, they cannot—if the theory is correct—change the general course or enable one institution to develop unilaterally relative to the others.[26]

25. Frank W. Young and Ruth C. Young, "Toward a Theory of Community Development," *Social Problems of Development and Urbanization,* VII, United Nations Conference on the Application of Science and Technology for the Benefit of the Less Developed Areas (Washington, D. C., 1963), 24–27.

26. Young and Young, 29.

Whether communities actually do follow some predetermined growth cycle as does a biological organism remains to be tested more fully. But unless community development theory is related closely to productive hypotheses about the community as a social unit, it is shaky at best.

Theory can be advanced in another direction, that is, by looking at community development programs themselves as systems of social action and thereby learning how they resemble and differ from other systems of action that may not have so marked a locality base.[27] The long lists of principles, based largely on one individual's experience, can then be put into some conceptual context and stated as operational propositions subject to careful test. Those "principles" which are contributing to a false mythology surrounding community development may be discarded; others may be kept and refined.

27. Irwin T. Sanders, "Community Development Programs in Sociological Perspective," in James H. Copp, ed., *Our Changing Rural Society: Perspectives and Trends* (Ames: The Iowa State University Press, 1964), 307–32.

CHAPTER 2

The Context of Community Development

R O L A N D   L.   W A R R E N

In considering the context of community development, one faces the alternatives of relating the analysis to the particular circumstances of one's own country or of keeping the analysis, insofar as possible, at a level that is more generally applicable. This chapter centers on the latter alternative, partly because community development is a widely applied method of bringing about social change that extends beyond the United States, and partly because, by dealing with the contextual considerations in more general terms, one is more likely to avoid myopic, situation-bound considerations of limited usefulness and is free to emphasize those contextual aspects which are relevant to all community development. In bridging the gap between the general considerations and the specific American context at this particular moment, the creativity of the reader is invited.

COMMUNITY DEVELOPMENT AND SOCIAL CHANGE

As a method for bringing about social change, community development serves alike in situations that are predominantly rural and preindustrial and in situations that are urban and industrialized. It is a means for promoting industrialization as well as for coping with its consequences. It applies to the needs of remote villages of traditionally agricultural countries and to those of the turbulent metropolises of highly industrialized countries. From these applications, it would appear that community development is being asked to bring about a set of conditions—roughly, "modernization"—and then being asked

Support of the research for this paper came through a Public Health Service research career program awarded (number K3–MH–21, 869) from the National Institute of Mental Health and supplementary grant number MH–11085–02.

to cope with the conditions modernization has created. Let us examine this paradoxical situation.

As indicated in the preceding chapter, community development is a method for bringing about change. But change is taking place anyway, both in highly industrialized countries and in the less industrialized ones. The vast changes that are taking place—the population explosion, the "revolution of rising expectations," the establishment of new nation-states, the flight from the land, the growth of cities, the growth of industries, the development of new technologies—all these changes and others as well, are subject to varying amounts of deliberate control, whether at the national level or at the community level.

In many countries, including the new nations with a scarcity of accessible resources as well as the socialist countries with nationalized resources, the deliberate attempt to control or at least to channel or influence these social changes takes place within the framework of a national plan. The framework organizes a variety of governmental efforts into a design to achieve a set of economic and social objectives. In the United States, on the other hand, a plurality of planning organizations, both governmental and nongovernmental, devise programs at various levels of geographic inclusiveness, and the results of their efforts seldom come into direct and deliberate correspondence with each other. Obviously, a wide range of variation exists among different countries as to the degree of centralization or decentralization of the planning, both geographic and functional, which affects fields such as health, education, economic development, and so on.

A widely used classification of these various attempts at deliberate control or influence over change is threefold: *economic, physical,* and *social* development or planning. Both the terms *development* and *planning* carry with them the connotation of a deliberate attempt to influence the course of events, with development implying the growth of some situation or condition as well as the implication of deliberate influence or control. Waterston has combined the terms in his concept of development planning:

> A country was considered to be engaged in development planning if its government made a deliberate and continuing attempt to accelerate the rate of economic and social progress and to alter institutional arrangements which were considered to block the attainment of this goal. The attempt had to be a conscious one made by a government and it had to be made often enough to give substance to the government's claim or belief that it was concerting policies and taking action designed to bring about economic and social progress and institutional change.[1]

Such development planning usually has economic, physical, and social aspects, each of which may be subject to separate explicit formulation. Community development is sometimes viewed as the local counterpart of such national development planning and may be incorporated into the national plan as a means of achieving certain specific results. On the other hand, it may be viewed quite apart from any national development plan, simply as a means of bringing about desired change at the local level. In some instances, the effort may affect a single locality; in others, it may be quite minimal, affecting only a small proportion of local people and a narrow range of activities and concern.

To summarize, community development is an attempt to influence the course of developmental changes at the community level. It may occur as part of a national plan or quite separately, and it occurs in the most varied settings—rural and urban, highly industrial or preindustrial. It may be a means to help bring about industrialization, or it may be a means to cope with its effects, or both simultaneously.

SWEEPING CHANGES OCCURRING THROUGHOUT MOST OF THE WORLD. In order to consider more systematically the context in which community development occurs, let us enumerate a number of the sweeping changes that are taking place in most parts of the world and then relate community development efforts to these changes:

1. Albert Waterston, *Development Planning: Lessons of Experience* (Baltimore: The Johns Hopkins Press, 1965), 21.

1. The increase in population.
2. The movement of people to the cities.
3. The growth of cities and the spread of urban ways to the countryside.
4. The growth of industrial production and the switch to nonagricultural pursuits.
5. The division of labor and consequent multiplication of occupations.
6. The development of large-scale organizations, not only in government and industry, but also in labor unions, voluntary associations, educational organizations, political parties, and so on.

More or less closely associated with these basic changes are others that, in a certain sense, are responses or adaptations to the changed conditions brought about by the above:

7. The development of modes of association based on rules and regulations, contract, formal organization, and comparative anonymity rather than on custom, face-to-face relations, common pursuits, homogeneity, and shared values.
8. Changes in the structure of family living and in the roles of husband and wife with respect to each other and their children, and of the members of this nuclear family unit to other kin.
9. The decline of the locality as a focus of association and the growth of other foci of association, such as employment in the same company or membership in the same union, or religious organization, or interest group.

All of these changes are interrelated in various ways. It is significant that, although these changes have occurred in various countries in different sequences and at different rates and thus are all apparent in different degrees at any one time, their operation is noticeable in countries that are diverse in geographic location or extent of development.

As an indication of the world-wide prevalence of the trends listed above, a group of national delegates from all parts of the world came together recently to discuss "Urban Development—Its Implications for Social Welfare." The group had for reference reports from national committees of 27 countries.

Although the reports revealed vast differences in the conditions within the various countries, they all reflected the operation of the interrelated combination of these same trends.[2]

For purposes of the present discussion, a brief designation is necessary for referring to these changes. I shall employ a term found useful elsewhere to denote a somewhat similar list of important social changes, referring to them in aggregate as *the great change*.[3]

It is helpful to relate community development to this great change. The context within which community development occurs is significantly different, depending on the extent to which the particular country or region has undergone one or another or several aspects of the great change. At the one extreme are the countries that are generally described as "highly developed," or "highly industrialized";[4] at the other are the countries that are called "less developed," or "under-industrialized." In each case, the meaning usually given to these terms is broad and denotes the scope of the trends in the great change.

Community development, in the decade or two after World War II, was thought of primarily as needed and taking place in the less developed countries, or in the less developed regions of the industrial countries. Thus, it was also considered primarily as needed in the smaller and more rural communities. Indeed, much of the thinking that has surrounded the concept of the community as a locality group has been cast in terms, essentially, of the smaller, rural communities. Baker Brownell, for example, writes: "A community is a group of people who know one another well. But this is satisfactory only when 'knowing well' means the full pattern of functional and social relationships which people may have with one another."[5] Ob-

2. *Urban Development—Its Implications for Social Welfare*, Report of Pre-Conference Working Party, 13th International Conference of Social Work (Washington, D. C., 1966).

3. Roland L. Warren, *The Community in America*, Chap. 3.

4. Unless otherwise indicated, the terms *developed, more developed, industrialized, highly industrialized* are used interchangeably, as are their opposites. Their use is not evaluative. Where a distinction is necessary, *developed* is more inclusive than *industrialized*.

5. Baker Brownell, *The Human Community: Its Philosophy and Practice for a Time of Crisis* (New York: Harper & Bros., 1950), 198.

viously, this is possible only in a small community. Brownell is consistent in drawing the implication: "The great city rises; the human community declines."[6]

Earlier, Arthur E. Morgan had observed: "If the numbers are too large, either community relationships will be restricted and more formal, or the community will break down into aggregates made up of several partial communities, often along economic or other class lines, and the total unity of the community will be partially lost."[7] He added, however, "Nevertheless, techniques and methods for developing some characteristics of community in larger populations can be developed,"[8] and, of course, this is precisely the function community development has been expected to perform in urban settings.[9]

THE LESS DEVELOPED CONTEXT.   Let us first consider community development in areas that have experienced the great change in only a modest degree. Here we study the so-called less developed countries, but also certain still largely rural, relatively isolated parts of the more developed countries, such as the Appalachian Region in the United States. Community development applies to these underdeveloped areas in two ways, namely, as a means of encouraging the great change and as a response to problems already brought about or anticipated by such changes as are occurring. Typically, both encouragement and response combine in any particular instance, but for purposes of analysis let us consider them separately.

In communities such as we are considering, plans for their development are typically directed at creating a sound industrial base and integrating the community with the larger society. The plans also involve the diffusion of new institutions and technical procedures to the people of the locality. Hence, the specific programs aim at increasing literacy, developing an

6. Brownell, 289.

7. Arthur E. Morgan, *The Small Community: Foundation of Democratic Life* (New York: Harper & Bros., 1942), 124.

8. Morgan, 124–25.

9. For an extensive treatment of the urban community development context, see Marshall B. Clinard, *Slums and Community Development: Experiments in Self Help.*

industrial base that requires greater specialization of production and results in greater interdependence with other communities, developing a sense of participation not only in the local institutions but also in the national political arena, importing economic and social resources from outside the community, introducing new health practices, and, withal, stimulating organized ways of problem-solving among the local people. Such activities are necessary prerequisites to the great change and to such advantages (longer life, higher real income, better nutrition and health) as the great change may bring about. In this context, community development can be seen as a means of achieving and guiding the great change—ideally, of guiding it along lines indicated by local values.

Often, though, the context is somewhat different. Many of these underdeveloped communities are already being affected by the great change (especially the growth of industries, the division of labor, the breakdown of older family and other institutional patterns), and the emphasis must be on coping with the problems the great change is bringing with it. As indicated earlier, much of this change may be quite unplanned and, indeed, may be apparently inexorable, while some of it may be the deliberate result of governmental policy. In any case, the context is essentially the same. The problem is to find ways through which local action can be taken to avoid some of the more disastrous results of the strains placed on time-worn institutions by modern circumstances.

We have separated the two conditions—encouragement and response—for purposes of analysis, but they usually appear together in the actual situation. Hence, we can summarize this first context for community development by saying that it is a context at the early stage of the great change, one in which the problem is to induce the great change as well as to help in the process of coping with its first effects.

It should be noted that not all community development in less developed countries is confined to rural communities. As the great change begins to affect the country, there is often a mushrooming of city populations, caused largely by migration from the rural areas. Vast numbers of people come to the cities, which do not have the economic base to afford the new arrivals adequate employment and cannot provide the educational, health, and welfare facilities they need. This has become an especially poignant and also especially frustrating circumstance for workers in community development.

It should be noted that developmental efforts of the type described above are appropriate also for many communities in the more developed countries that have perhaps had at one time a more viable economic and social base than they have at present. The decline or moving away of industries, such as mining or textile manufacturing, may leave communities with grave problems resulting from the lack of an economic base as well as the concomitant widespread apathy and discouragement. The employment of community development as a means of bettering the community's economic base thus becomes appropriate.[10]

THE MORE DEVELOPED CONTEXT.   Let us turn now to the context for community development at the other end of the spectrum of great change—in the highly urban, highly industrial countries. In these countries, the various processes listed earlier as constituting the great change have run a considerable course. As an example, let us examine a large American city, along with its metropolitan area. Division of labor is highly intricate, with literally thousands of different occupations. Gainful occupations are organized into industrial companies or smaller entrepreneurs, governmental and nongovernmental organizations, all providing a highly complex network of production and distribution within the city and in exchange for the produce of other cities. The institutional structure is highly developed, and education, welfare, and health agencies may be so numerous that their coordination and utilization for optimum benefit present administrative problems.

A series of structural and personal conditions also present problems. On the structural level, there is the necessity for a viable economic base that provides employment opportunities for all and for an assessed valuation high enough to yield the

10. Bruyn makes an extensive analysis of one such effort in the cases analyzed in his book. See Severyn T. Bruyn, *Communities in Action: Patterns and Process.*

real estate taxes needed to support public services on an adequate level. Along with these needs rides the whole complex of problems resulting from the flight to the suburbs and the ghettoizing of the city center: the traffic congestion caused by flow to and from the suburbs; the inadequacy of city services due to falling land values and taxes in the ghetto area; the lack of middle-income housing; and so on through a long list.

On the personal level, there are problems of unemployment, disabilities, marital discord, family conflict, juvenile delinquency, drug addiction, crime, and on through another long list. Needless to say, all these personal problems have important structural aspects as well.

But these problems, structural and personal, cannot be solved by accelerating the great change. Quite to the contrary: These problems are all related more or less closely to the impact of the great change. The great change is actually part of the problem, rather than part of the solution.

In the broadest sense, community development is concerned in this context, as well, and with a method through which people can come to confront their problems in a concerted way, using such resources as are available, whether from within the community or from outside. In the United States, these resources are available most spectacularly in the form of huge grants-in-aid from the federal government for various carefully delineated programs.

But in the larger cities, the opportunity for face-to-face interaction of any substantial proportion of the population in a process of confronting any substantial proportion of its problems is mathematically impossible. Problems must be confronted by delegation, and these confrontations take place within the rubric of large-scale organizations such as boards of education and schools, chambers of commerce and business and industrial companies, welfare councils and social agencies, the municipal government and its various departments, and so on.

The most broadly developed professional rubrics for bringing together such organizations have developed primarily in the field of social welfare agencies under the name of *community organization*. Actually, in the larger cities, there is no single rubric within which these varied organizations are co-ordinated. Rather, various segments of organizational activity —education, social services, health services, and economic activity—are loosely coordinated in a number of separate organizations. These large-scale coordinating organizations form part of a competitive arena in which they act more or less autonomously with respect to each other, meanwhile achieving varying degrees of coordination within their own special fields of activity. No way has yet been devised for engaging large numbers of people at any significant level of participation along the whole gamut of community concerns.

Hence, in the larger, more complex urban setting, community development must take one of two forms. Either it operates at the level of the organization and the super-organization, failing to engage the vast majority of the people in any meaningful way, or it restricts its field of operations to an extremely narrow segment of the total community picture, such as betterment of schools or improvement of street cleaning—and then only sporadically—or it takes place within the various subcommunities, which are small enough in scale to afford a basis for broad, meaningful involvement.

Such effort at the subcommunity level has usually taken two forms. One is that of the usual neighborhood association, an attempt to organize people in a small part of the city for confronting the problems and exploiting the possibilities that are appropriate to their neighborhood. Such associations are usually interested in school facilities, parks and recreational space, the condition of the streets, police protection, and a number of other concerns of immediate relevance to the people of the neighborhood. Attempts to interest such associations in the larger problems of the surrounding city or of the larger society have usually met with only minimal success or total failure. At the level of neighborhood problems, however, they have proved in many instances to be capable of effective and sustained activity.

The other form such neighborhood activity has taken in the United States has developed more recently: the creation of neighborhood organizations not so much to confront the immediate problems of the neighborhood as to confront the larger social structure in which these neighborhood problems are generated. These attempts to "organize the poor" take place on a neighborhood level, but they have implications for the structure of the city and of the larger society. One way of looking at them is to say that they are attempts to accomplish three interrelated purposes: to organize the poor for action on their own behalf; to develop a "position" or a series of specific proposals; and to make these positions and proposals known in the larger councils where the affairs of the city are considered.

The rationale underlying such activity is that formerly the poor have not been represented in any effective sense, as indicated by the tendency of social service agencies to place greater emphasis on middle-class clients, and the general neglect of the physical, social, and educational aspects of poor neighborhoods. If the poor are to participate meaningfully in the life of the larger society, they must have a "position." This can be developed only as they discuss their situation and form their points of view in interaction with their peers. Next, these points of view must be presented in the councils of the community, which can be done only if there is sufficient organization to select representatives who are legitimated to "speak for" them. And finally, their position will be given weight in the community's decision-making only if their spokesmen are backed by some form of power, power that can come only through organization and the capacity to take concerted action, whether this be in lobbying, education, protesting, or voting.

To convert poor neighborhoods into effective subcommunities is not an easy or simple task; it is one of the most challenging problems confronting community development in urban areas.

To summarize: In the more developed countries, which have experienced the great change in a large degree, community development is confronted with a different kind of context. Here, the problems that communities face are problems that are themselves concomitants of the great change. These problems, too, are economic, physical, and social in nature. But in the more developed countries, community development efforts are directed largely at taking effective adaptive action to mitigate the painful consequences of the great change, rather than at bringing about that change. The great change has disrupted older patterns of social relations, and that disruption in turn has brought about adaptive behavior that is experienced as the structural and personal stresses of urban industrial life. Action to mitigate these stresses in urban communities is possible for only a small proportion of the people, acting through various relatively fragmented organizations. This fragmentary action affords at least a modicum of deliberate, coordinated problem-solving activity, but it does not resolve the question of how a substantial proportion of the population can meaningfully and effectively be brought into the process. At the neighborhood level, however, community development efforts can engage a large proportion of individuals over a broader sweep of neighborhood-level issues. Neighborhood-level development has recently come into special prominence because of its utilization as a method for helping the poor to organize themselves so that they can have a voice and exercise power in the community arena.

THE RELEVANCE OF THE COMMUNITY LEVEL. As is pointed out in Chapter 5 of this book, community development is viewed not only as a means of accomplishing certain specific program objectives, but it is also considered intrinsically valuable as a process. It is not merely a question of what is accomplished, but of how it is accomplished. Community development is often thought of as crucial, on the basis of a number of specific affirmations:

A healthy society is the product of healthy, vigorous communities.

It is better for community people to plan and work for the things they want in their community than to have them "handed down" by a higher governmental authority.

Participation in the development of the community is an important preventive for the alienation of individuals in the "mass society" over which they have no control and in which they feel no meaningful sense of participation.

Strong participation in community affairs is a necessary basis for a democratic society.

Nevertheless, our analysis of the contexts of community development shows that, as the great change progresses and as communities become, not more self-sufficient, but less self-sufficient and more closely intertwined with the major institutions of the larger society, fewer of the problems people face in their communities can be adequately confronted at the community level. The population explosion, the growth of nationhood, the struggles among nations, the broad ideological currents that engulf the world, to say nothing of questions of national prosperity, employment opportunity, the availability of capital for growth and of consumer goods for current standards of living—none of these is subject to control by any one community.

There has been no let-up in the pace at which large-scale organizations are growing and decision-making is becoming centralized at levels more inclusive than the community. Even in those Eastern European countries which are now adopting the economic policy of Libermanism[11] and which are, as a deliberate policy change, decentralizing some of their formerly centralized national planning—even here the trend does not seem to be in the direction of dispersing the decision-making function to the community. Rather, the process is one of functional decentralization—by industries and industrial units that, in the most democratic form, are under the jurisdiction of workers but not the whole community, and by regions rather than by communities. Elsewhere, the trend toward centralization increases.

Thus, at the same time that community development is promoted as desirable for a democratic society, much of the basis for it is suffering attrition through the increasing extent to which the community affairs of people are influenced by events and decisions at regional or national or international levels. A number of aspects of this situation can be given brief consideration here:

First, it is interesting to observe that what seems to be happening is a gradual switch in emphasis, particularly in the de-

11. The Russian economist Evsei Liberman advocates decentralization of decision-making by placing the power to decide in the hands of socialist enterprises rather than in the Central Committee. His policy also advocates greater use of profit incentives in Eastern European markets.

veloping countries, to the concept of social development rather than to community development. The two are by no means mutually exclusive, but the growth in importance of social development is in part, at least, realization that "what happens to people" as distinguished from the accomplishment of certain task objectives is not solely a matter of community development but involves regional and national action as well, and that many of the institutions people need for a more satisfactory life must be initiated at national or regional levels rather than at the community level.

Second, there appears to be growing recognition that participation at the community level is not the only alternative to alienation in the mass society. As William Kornhauser points out, the need is for participation at levels intermediate between the individual and the large-scale organizations of the mass society.[12] Traditionally, such participation has taken place principally on the basis of locality. But such participation can also occur functionally, in labor unions, political parties, interest groups, religious organizations, and economic activity at various levels—some less inclusive than the community and some more inclusive. There would seem to be no compelling reason why the local community, as such, should provide the only opportunities for social participation.

Finally, even though many functions are not appropriate for community-level participation, many others still are, and presumably will be for the predictable future. Certain locally oriented functions apparently need to be performed on the scene where people live, and the people who live in any locality share a common interest in seeing that these functions are performed satisfactorily. Stores must be available to people where they live, as must primary schools, streets, police and fire protection, and a number of other readily identifiable facilities or services. People who live in a particular locality have a common interest in these locally oriented functions, even though they do not especially care about associating with each other in their leisure time. They may have diverse individual interests and

12. William Kornhauser, *The Politics of Mass Society* (Glencoe, Ill.: The Free Press of Glencoe, 1959).

positions that, in many cases, orient them more forcibly toward regional or national groups than toward their neighbors.

There can be no single answer to the question of what is a relevant basis for community organization and interaction around such common interests. In some communities and in some neighborhoods of large cities, the degree of identification with other people in the locality may remain at a minimum without catastrophic results. In other cases, the viability of the neighborhood as a satisfactory environment in which to live may depend on the residents coming together on the basis of locality and organizing themselves to confront their problems.

In sum, from the social context alone, there can be no single clear answer to the question of how important it is that people organize themselves strongly on the basis of locality. The answer must be considered as a variable, to be assessed differently in the multitude of different situations and conditions that surround the lives of people in various communities.

REGIONAL AND NATIONAL RELATIONSHIPS. From the foregoing analysis, the close interrelationship of community problems and the conditions of the region and the nation become apparent. The relationships are reciprocal. Conditions in the region and nation place limits on the setting within which community development occurs. To paraphrase John Donne, no community is an island. Every community needs resources—economic, technical, often political—from the surrounding countryside. Likewise, every community is affected by the economic, technical, and political conditions that exist in the surrounding region and nation. At the same time, conditions in individual communities affect the well-being of the surrounding region and nation. From this relationship the practical problem arises: To what extent will community development efforts in the region or nation be coordinated in order to bring those areas' resources to bear more directly on the local communities? To what extent will the programs of the local communities be coordinated to bring optimal benefit to the region and nation?

One of the difficulties of organizing the regional aspects of community development is the fact that the most appropriate regional division for one purpose—say, industry—may differ from that for another purpose—say, elementary education. These functional divisions, in turn, may differ from political boundaries of regions. This difference may be true of the immediate area surrounding a city—the immediate urbanized region —or it may be true of a larger political subdivision, such as the county, state, province, and so on. For our present purposes, we can use the term *region* most broadly, including any or all of these as the context demands—some geographic district larger than the municipality but smaller than the entire country.

This surfeit of different (but appropriate) regions is quite apparent in the United States. One of the most problematic instances is the metropolitan region surrounding large American cities and including suburban communities. Ecologically and economically, these areas are interdependent with the metropolitan center; in actuality, no political entity corresponds to this metropolitan complex. There is the large city; there are the surrounding smaller cities, towns, and villages; there are numerous special districts; there are counties. But there is no governmental decision-making apparatus with tax power and with legal authority to administer the affairs of this urban complex, nor is there any likelihood of the formation in the near future of such an inclusive governmental unit with appropriate powers.

One need only mention the fact that many concerns of large cities, such as commuter transit, land-use patterns of the metropolitan area, highway and bridge authorities, are not only intercommunity, but interstate. On the state level, as well, problems in various functional areas do not coincide with state boundaries, and there is no existing governmental organization appropriate to the level at which the problems must be confronted. On the federal level, the many different groupings of states into regions for purposes of banking and finance, census, and the regional administration of various federal agency programs likewise illustrate the lack of correspondence between functional areas and geographic governmental jurisdictions.

This "crazy-quilt" pattern of functional regions helps account for the lack of organization of the various geographic regions for regional development and planning. It also helps to explain the great multiplicity of special districts—*ad hoc* governmental districts with limited power (often, however, including taxing power) set up for the performance of specific functions, such as water districts, sewage districts, school districts, and so on. At a different level, it is a commonplace that the district offices of state governments often are not only divided into geographic areas that do not coincide, but also that district-level offices are seldom brought into any meaningful coordination with each other. Much the same situation exists among the regional offices of the federal government.

This confused and apparently uncoordinated situation should not be taken *ipso facto* as undesirable. The problems just discussed are virtually insuperable in any fundamental sense, simply because the functional areas do not coincide geographically. The most effective action is to make an optimal resolution of the problems of regional districting and coordination. The costs in time and effort and other resources of setting up regional systems that would coordinate the various functional divisions at all appropriate geographic levels would very possibly be much greater than the benefits. This is not to say, however, that the existing "mix" is optimal.

REGIONAL AND NATIONAL ASPECTS OF COMMUNITY DEVELOPMENT. The preceding discussion constitutes a good backdrop against which to place a complaint made frequently by those interested in community development work at the community level in the United States. At the same time that the federal government is making new resources available to communities, each new federal program sets up its own goals and its own administrative machinery and its own constraints on the local community. Coordination of federal policies in relation to the specific community and its special circumstances would seem to be desirable at the community level. Yet, the different federal agencies working in the community are so organized that they are relatively isolated from each other. Each is encapsulated in its own administrative hierarchy, which leads through regional offices to Washington. Each is part of a different federal administrative apparatus based on different federal legislation. Under these circumstances, their functional coordination at the municipal level, though highly desirable, is extremely difficult. Attempts toward coordination will no doubt succeed in the next decade, these attempts being based on the increasing clamor from the cities. One such attempt—confined, to be sure, to the Department of Housing and Urban Development—is that of the establishment of urban representatives, or expediters, in different cities to help coordinate the numerous federal housing programs, especially those within the purview of the Department of Housing and Urban Development.

A second major consideration in the regional and national programs of community development is the extent to which goals and programs should be set at the regional or national level and the extent to which they should be set at the community level. Many issues are involved in this large question, not the least of which is that the record of experience of local community initiative in such matters as health and welfare and educational services is that initiative should not rest with local people and that such federal funds as are made available should have reasonable limitations. The great impulse of federal initiative regarding local communities has arisen from a number of different sources. Important among these is the inadequate fiscal base for community support of the costly undertakings that are needed (urban renewal, school improvement, housing, etc.). Further, communities are often stingy and backward in the programs they are prepared to develop to resolve such problems as housing, racial integration, urban renewal, schools, pollution, health care, and so on. A combination of stimulus and constraint from outside the communities is therefore needed if anything more than sporadic progress is desired.

On the other hand, however, the communities should be able to modify federal programs in ways that adapt them to the local situations. Often, local programs are based more on the availability of federal funds for specific purposes than on the community's conviction that these programs are the ones most needed.

Chapter 3 of this book discusses the extent to which community development goals and programs should be locally determined or should be determined in part or in whole by "experts" or by regional or national governmental or nongovernmental organizations. The purpose of the brief discussion here has been to describe the setting that creates these issues and makes them extremely difficult to resolve.

A third consideration regarding regional and national relationships requires only brief mention, although its great importance is apparent. As mentioned in an earlier section, many of the most vital problems communities face are not resolvable at the community level. This is true of regional and national economic conditions, questions of war and peace, which have the most fateful consequences for community living, and questions of quite a different nature, such as the population explosion, the development of science and technology, the migration of people to the cities, and so on.

In sum, many types of activity are more appropriate for the national or regional level than for the community level, but difficulties in coordination at national and regional levels are numerous. These difficulties are various, some purely administrative, others the results of the apparently unalterable fact that functional areas do not always coincide geographically with each other or with governmental jurisdictions, still others the products of the inappropriateness of the community level for confronting certain problems. These difficulties, in addition to the reticence and conservatism of many communities when confronting their problems in a systematic way, form a complex background against which decisions must be made. That these decisions govern the way in which regional and national programs are to be structured and the scope of the decision-making and operation that are to be allocated to national, regional, and community levels, respectively, raises these local attitudes to the first importance.

OTHER ASPECTS OF THE COMMUNITY DEVELOPMENT CONTEXT. This chapter has considered some of the broader aspects of the context of community development, with primary emphasis on the relation of community development to the great change and on the respective roles for community level action as distinguished from regional and national levels. Yet, specific contexts for community development show extreme variation, and these differences must be taken into account in planning or operating or assessing specific community development endeavors. I shall consider a few of these variations in this concluding section.

The most obvious variation has already been mentioned—the degree of "modernization," or extent to which the community has experienced the great change. If one compares the effort at community development within a large modern metropolis with that of a remote agricultural village in one of the less developed countries, a number of important and possibly crucial differences may be apparent: level of literacy and education, experience with democratic institutions, availability of financial and personnel resources, and so on, all of which would have to be considered in adopting appropriate methods and strategies.

Another important variation is in the number of potential sources or sponsors of community development efforts. In some countries, these may be restricted to the specific organization for community development that is included in the national plan. Little else can be counted on for assistance, except for the sporadic ventures into community development by a religious or other nongovernmental organization. In other countries, the sources of sponsorship and of personnel to help stimulate community development may be extremely numerous, including not only a number of different (and often competing) programs of various departments and ministries, but also state or provincial efforts, which also may be numerous, as well as university extension, national, state, or local voluntary associations, including religious organizations, and efforts sponsored by industrial companies.

A related consideration is the extent to which these various efforts are related in any specific way to the governmental structure. In some settings they are not only largely governmental, but actually part of a deliberate national, more or less integrated plan. At the other extreme, they may have little relation to government, being quite independently sponsored, organized, and financed, and they may look to various levels and branches of government, if at all, solely as sources of financial or personnel resources.

Another type of variation has to do with whether the sponsoring agency is roughly a single-purpose or a multipurpose organization. In countries where numerous agencies are active at the community level, many of them are engaging in community development as a means for developing local programs in their own particular area of interest, be this health, education, urban renewal, housing, prevention of juvenile delinquency, or whatever. Thus, according to the sponsorship, such efforts may be perceived as stretching across the entire spectrum of possible community concerns or as being concentrated in only one predetermined field of interest. In the latter circumstance, there is much more likelihood that goals will be primarily determined by a specific organization—whether within or outside of the community—rather than by the people who are the participant-targets of the program.

Another obvious variation is in the size and complexity of the community within which community development occurs. Although other variables may affect the picture, it is perhaps safe to generalize that the larger in size and complexity the community that is chosen as a unit for development, the less proportion of the total population will be involved in it in any direct way, and the greater the number of organizations that are party to the process. In large cities, where the whole city is considered as the community to be developed, procedures will therefore differ drastically from the concept of direct, face-to-face interaction by all the citizens. Thus, those who claim this last characteristic to be an essential ingredient of the community development method may challenge whether community development in the strict sense is possible except in smaller units.

Because of the importance of such variations as these, there can be no simple recipe or formula for community development. Community development endeavors can be expected to vary infinitely, on the basis of the contextual matters that have been discussed in this chapter. They will also vary in the values people apply as guides to the selection of their goals and to the determination of their methods.

PART Two   The Community
Development Process and Its Implications

The next three chapters consider the community development process itself and examine the sociological and psychological implications of the process. In Chapter 3, Sutton describes the fullest achievement of the community development process as the establishment and maintenance of a social system addressing itself to continuing improvement action episodes relevant to a community. The relative infrequency of this occurring is the major theme of Sutton's sociological analysis. He identifies three elements that together constitute an action episode: a value-goal component; a social organizational component; and a temporal component.

Three of the dimensions of the value-goal component are the relationship that is preserved between the goals of the action episode and the values of society, the balance between task goals and group maintenance goals, and the degree to which action episode goals agree with the society's general welfare. Two basic dimensions in the social organizational component are the indigenous recognition of the organization as legitimate and representative, and the maintenance of constructive relationships between the organization and various other organizations and administrative echelons. The temporal component involves not just time per se, but the order and sequence of events as well. Sutton notes the difficulties faced by the community developer in the slow pace and long duration of many action episodes. He suggests that, to facilitate the community development process, we must first find ways by which the essentials of previous actions can be reviewed and made relevant for emerging phases, and second, we must promote more realistic attitudes toward the slow pace of most community action.

Sutton's concept of action episodes provides a useful analytical device for viewing community development as a series of process or basic units. The linkage of a series of these units creates the continuity that is so essential in the process. Viewed in these terms, the process becomes more adaptable to empirical research.

Haggstrom distinguishes between the object community and the acting community in his discussion of the psychological implications of the community development process. As an object, the community is made up of an interdependent system of neighborhoods, interest groups, and other subsystems. As an acting community, it engages in collective action and community decision-making. People and groups of the object community have differential access to the acting community. In fact, not all marginal groups that seek to enter the acting community are allowed to do so. Haggstrom suggests that the poor, Negroes, children, and other entire categories of the population are outsiders who seldom enter the acting community.

This discussion leads to the consideration of two major varieties of community development. The first, and more traditional, process is the internal development of the acting community in the object community. The second, which Haggstrom sees as the central concern for community development in the United States today, is the development of the object community into the acting community through a process whereby marginal groups no longer remain marginal. The problem is how to achieve incorporation of such groups into the acting community in modern industrial society.

Much of what Haggstrom has to say raises valid questions, particularly in relation to the community developer and his professional role. His discussion of community development as a process by which marginal groups migrate into the acting community offers one of the clearest theoretical statements on the so-called conflict or protest approach. This chapter also identifies a key concept in development efforts that is frequently overlooked or ignored. Since the goal of the development process is for marginal groups to enter the acting community, the long-range objective is to make the community development process much more inclusive and the outcome of the process determined by and relevant to most all groups in the community. When this objective is reached, using Haggstrom's terms, the object and acting community will coincide.

Is this goal attainable? Haggstrom suggests the odds against it are not as great as might be supposed. He cites the ability of organizations of marginal people to initiate and control brief encounters with the acting community. Major changes for marginal people can be carried out at little cost to the community, and the frequent underestimation of the ability of marginal people by the acting community gives the marginal groups a tactical advantage.

Haggstrom concludes his presentation with an overview of the psychology of the organizational process and a final note on evaluation. It is here that he distinguishes *authentic* community development from other efforts that carry the same name. The distinction, according to Haggstrom, is whether the process is aimed at promoting and rationalizing already formulated policies and programs or whether it focuses on the community's interests and concerns as they emerge. A distinction also lies in whether activities are uncritically entered into or if serious consideration is given to whether proposed programs will actually help to develop the community.

A general outline of the community development process is the major thrust of Schler's chapter. The three interrelated dimensions of the process, in Schler's model, are the *procedural*, the *content*, and the *human interaction* dimensions. The four stages through which the process moves are those of resource organization, the engagement of resource system with a community unit, the activating a local goal-orientated system, and operation of the local system. Phases within each of the four stages are outlined for each of the three dimensions of the process and then briefly discussed.

In a final portion of the chapter, Schler discusses a generally accepted set of traditions or basic tendencies that are emphasized in the community development process. Along with Sanders, he hesitates to endorse such tendencies as principles. In the Introduction, the term *basic elements* was employed to cover much the same content. The five tendencies delineated by Schler are: (1) toward prospective goal setting; (2) toward self-help and self-development; (3) toward the democratization of human relationships; (4) toward rationality in decision-making; and (5) toward concerted decision-making and action systems.

The chapters by Sutton, Haggstrom, and Schler provide a broad view of the process we call community development. They offer several theoretical frameworks within which a more extensive practice theory can be specified. The three authors also raise a number of serious questions and dilemmas that must be faced by this emerging field of specialists. Some of these issues and implications of process comprise the final chapter of this book.

CHAPTER 3

The Sociological Implications
of the Community Development Process

WILLIS A. SUTTON, JR.*

We conceive of community development as a continuity of complex action episodes in which the selection, planning, and achieving of goals are deliberate and oriented to the collective good of an entire place-related society.[1] This concept makes use of observations cast specifically in terms of process units of a size appropriate to the scale of societal development. By first clarifying its key referents, we can provide a framework for realistically assessing the sociological aspects of community development as an ongoing action process.

A complex action episode is any series of interaction events integrated and bounded by a common close relevance to some question, problem, or item of collective interest to a relatively numerous set of persons comprising the main decision-makers in the events.[2] Such episodes constitute observable units of nat-

---

*The author wishes to express his appreciation for the helpful comments on an earlier version of this chapter by his colleagues Thomas R. Ford and John B. Stephenson.

1. This essay is not the place for an extended discussion of the nature or implications of different definitions of community development. I believe, however, that my definition incorporates most of the more salient features of the most widely used characterizations, nearly all of which state or imply that community development is a process. In the framework of this definition, a set of action episodes provides a focus more adaptable to empirical inquiry. Most concepts utilize the wholistic perspective as an important trait; a number of them emphasize the combination of lay or citizen participation with special technical or professional help, and a number imply the collaboration of indigenous with exogenous forces as an integral aspect of the process. We see these as an important means to continuity rather than as integral with it.

2. An "interaction event" is simply any unit of interaction in which the same participants carry on an uninterrupted encounter. We seek to contrast *complex* action episodes—those involving a number of actors over a considerable period of time in which there are a number of different

ural, large-scale social activity delimited by temporally identifiable points of origin, movement, and ending. Not all complex action episodes are relevant to community development, but such episodes are basic units in the process, and the principles discoverable in the interrelations among their events and participants are largely determinative of its character.[3]

Two special attributes mark the episodes that are components of community development: Deliberate planning of events plays an important though not necessarily determinative part in their course, and the items that integrate and determine their boundaries are among the collective concerns of some residential population. This latter attribute requires explanation.

This is best accomplished by drawing a clear distinction between *society*, and *community*—terms that have often been used to refer to essentially similar sets of phenomena. In this sense, *society* refers to the social space or context comprehensive of all the social activity of an area's resident population, including its range of institutions and all social interactions, while *community* is assumed to be simply a small-scale, local society.[4]

A different distinction, one having to do with the degree of

specific "encounters" or events—with *simple* ones of shorter duration and fewer actors. All Warren's "community action episodes" are of this complex variety. (See his *The Community in America*, 308.) "Community action courses" as developed by Willis A. Sutton, Jr., are also all complex action episodes. (See his "Community Action Conceptualization." A Survey of Past Efforts and a New Interactional Synthesis." University of Kentucky, 1964. Mimeographed.)

3. Of course, other approaches might be used for a sociological analysis of community development. They might, for example, be derived from social change, diffusion of ideas and practices, social participation, administration and organization theory, collective behavior, conflict, and social stratification.

4. See, for example, Arnold M. Rose, *Sociology* (New York: Alfred A. Knopf, Inc., 1956), 559 and 567; Leonard Broom and Phillip Selznick, *Sociology* (Evanston, Ill.: Row, Peterson and Company, 1955), 31; Robin Williams, *American Society* (New York: Alfred A. Knopf, Inc., 1951), 449; Irwin T. Sanders, *The Community: Introduction to a Social System*, 26 and 69; and on the concept *society*, Harry M. Johnson, *Sociology* (New York: Harcourt, Brace & World, Inc., 1960), 9–12.

comprehensiveness, seems helpful to our interests. Retaining the same concept of society, we suggest *community* be viewed as a particular part of society—its immediately common or collective life. It is contained within society and is moulded and conditioned by it, but it is a segment separately identifiable from society. *Community* is those parts of a resident society important to its unit or group concerns. Whatever developments require group decision or sanction, whatever happenings express unit loyalty or symbolize collective identity for a given resident population—these constitute *community*. *Community* is thus divested of its local connotation; its essence is not what is "local to," but rather what is "collective for" a resident population.[5]

In our view, neither the community's nor the society's referent should be limited to any particular unit of geography. Each is place-related, but the areal extent is not the differentiating attribute; each is equally applicable to the resident population of any geographic area of social significance. We may deal with local societies and communities, with state or regional societies and communities, and with national or international societies and communities—referring respectively, in each case, to wholes or to special collective segments of the residential population's social context.[6]

The process of community development is also applicable at different residency echelons. Whenever a continuity of conscious planning and operations by numbers of people is focused upon the questions of unit or collective interest for any resident population, we have an instance of community development.

5. It is to be noted that while this conception makes the community more circumscribed than society, it also shows why it is less immediately specifiable, more fluid in its constituency, and, thus, in some ways more tenuous. The great travail attendant upon efforts to arrive at a thoroughly useful conceptualization of community seems not unrelated to this quality.

6. This applicability of community to any geographic level is similar to the conception of community as any spatially contingent social system projected by Christen Jonassen. See his "Community Typology," in Marvin B. Sussman, ed., *Community Structure and Analysis* (New York: Thomas Y. Crowell Company, 1959), 15–36, especially 17–22. Jonassen does not deal with the concept *society*.

The geographic dimension, while operationally important, is not substantively distinctive. The generic social content may be manifest at any residential echelon.

The specification of the particular residential echelon of concern is of great importance in analyzing community development for this residential society, and its relations with other echelons provide the key reference points for understanding actors' orientations to, and motivations and authority for, the various decisions that comprise the episodes in the development process.

We now turn to the last of the key terms in our definition of community development. Using *continuity* as an integral phase of our concept means first that a minimum requirement for qualification as community development is some linkage of a series of communal action episodes.

Continuity also implies that the likelihood of additional successful constructive effort must be one of the primary considerations governing the orientations to action within any series of action episodes qualifying as community development. In this sense, community development is viewed as that execution and linkage of action episodes that enhances the probability of additional constructive, residential-group activity.

The epitome of the community development process lies in this idea of continuation. Its fullest achievement, at least in the sociological perspectives, involves the establishment and maintenance of a social system responsible for, and effective in, continuing improvement action episodes relevant to the collective life of a place-defined population.

The relative infrequency of achieving the ultimate goal of the process suggests the theme for this sociological analysis. What is the combination of factors that accounts for failure or, obversely, occasionally facilitates success in achieving this improvement system, allowing the continuity of development work?

An analysis of factors inhibiting and facilitating system development and maintenance can best be organized in terms of those elements which together constitute the structure of any complex action episode—the observational unit we have selected as most appropriate to the scale of residential development work. These elements are: a value-goal component made up of the objectives and rationale governing actions taken in the events; an organizational component constituted by the social fabric of persons and groups participating in the events; and a temporal component comprised of the sequential and concurrent patterning of the flow of events.[7]

While much of what will be said will apply to work at any residential echelon, the perspective assumed for the remaining discussion will be that of the professional worker seeking to analyze the aids and obstacles to community development continuity in action episodes oriented to a local community.

THE VALUE-GOAL COMPONENT

Whether action is focused upon establishing a new school tax rate, the building of a hospital, or the planning of an anniversary celebration, the course and outcome of a community action episode are heavily dependent upon the relationship existing between its goals and the values of the encompassing society. Fundamentally, these values are the basic assumptions

7. These divisions have been used by Sutton in the conceptualization and analysis of community action episodes. See his "Community Action Conceptualization: . . . ," and his "The Social Constituency of Community Activities: Comparisons from Three Kentucky Communities," mimeographed paper read before the meeting of the Rural Sociological Society, 1964, and his "Socio-Temporal Structure of Community Activities: Event and Episode Comparisons in Three Kentucky Towns," mimeographed paper read before the meeting of the Society for the Study of Social Problems, 1964.

The components are also implicit in other action literature. See Paul A. Miller, *Community Health Action, A Study of Community Contrast* (East Lansing: Michigan State College Press, 1953); James W. Green and Selz C. Mayo, "A Framework for Research in the Actions of Community Groups," *Social Forces*, 31 (May, 1953), 320–27; Christopher Sower and others, *Community Involvement* (Glencoe, Ill.: Free Press, 1957); Harold F. Kaufman, "Toward an Interactional Conception of Community," *Social Forces*, 38 (October, 1959), 8–17; Severyn T. Bruyn, *Communities in Action, Patterns and Process* (New Haven, Conn.: College & University Press, 1963), 135–57; Roland Warren, *The Community in America* (Chicago: Rand McNally & Company, 1963), 315–20; and George M. Beal and others, *Social Action and Interaction in Program Planning* (Ames: The Iowa State University Press, 1966), 54–92.

about the relative goodness or badness of things that tend to be uncritically used as criteria for and justification of action.

An understanding of the relationship between action episode goals and these values is crucial to development continuity, but the character of the relationship is not a simple one. We cannot say that continuity will always be served by a close alignment of goals with values. The specific discrepancies or conformations among particular values and goals within different types of situations must be considered. Certain values may be relevant mainly for certain goals; given certain goals, the salience of values may be heightened or diminished by a number of factors; and, over time and within the communal context, a balance between different type goals and an identification of goals with the public good may be especially strategic.

Activities of the immediate past always tend to increase the salience of some values and decrease the salience of others. To a considerable degree, values may be seen as precipitants of former actions.[8] Certainly value salience is, in part, a function of the degree of emotional commitment involved in recent collective activity. Soon after a bitter factional fight over the location of a new school, any slight implication of favor to either side may set off additional waves of rabid partisanship. But when the confrontation is ancient history, activities with far greater potential for stimulating conflict may hardly be noticed. This is not to suggest that conflict is bad, nor is it to imply that long-range developmental continuity is not often served by vigorous contest; it is, rather, to underline the need for considering the immediate past when assessing the salience of values for action episode goals.

The balance between task achievement goals and identity or group maintenance goals is also an important consideration.[9] Planning for achievement related to both of these goals must be systematic if continuity is to be attained. The neglect of either for any significant period will lead to costly disruptions. If attention is so riveted upon tasks—like the building of a new

8. See Solon T. Kimball, "Individualism and the Formation of Values," *Applied Behavioral Science*, 2 (Fall, 1966), 465–82, particularly 480.

9. See Roland Warren, *The Community in America*, 312.

school, the institution of sewer services, or the establishment of an antipoverty agency, however desirable in themselves—that emerging differences, injured pride, and hurt feelings are too long untended, the period of cumulative development will be relatively short. On the other hand, an excessive preoccupation with these interpersonal problems may be equally as dangerous to continuity, for task accomplishment is always a requirement for group morale. The precise way in which goals of both types can best be served in practical exigencies cannot be detailed. The difficulty of their balance may be greater in appearance than reality for, if it is virtually impossible to achieve task goals without some friction, task accomplishment itself is one of the keys to the maintenance of a development system. A careful combination of both goals within all action episodes may be effective in some cases. In another set of circumstances, however, a pattern of alternation might be best—one or two episodes oriented to task achievement, followed by other episodes directed mainly to group cohesion.

ACTION EPISODE GOALS AND THE COMMON GOOD. Another dimension of the value-goal component that is significant to development continuity is the degree to which action episode goals are shown to converge with those conditions that characterize the society's general welfare or common good. The character of the communal context embodying these improvement efforts greatly heightens the importance of this dimension. Contrasting these communal traits with those in the context surrounding action episodes within bureaucratic structures will sharpen the focus of this relationship.

Within a formal organization, persons take action as incumbents of roles having reasonably clear and widely recognized definitions. Relatively specific goals govern the relevance of factors that are permitted to influence decisions. A system of explicit rewards stimulates and reinforces conformity to major decisions. By the same token, the fear that these rewards might be lost strongly inhibits irresponsible acts.

In such circumstances the rationale for the proposals and decisions of leaders is clear and understandable. Because a definite set of identities and commitments—Coleman calls them "attachments"[10]—exists for each of the major actors in this formal context, the scope of relations that influence their policies is relatively narrow and widely shared. Correspondingly, the bases of evaluation open to those affected by these positions are considerably restricted.

Such conditions maximize stability and minimize friction, but even here, as Gouldner[11] has noted, tension develops whenever grounds emerge for believing that any of the principal actors' identities and commitments, which should remain irrelevant to organization decisions, actually influence their choices.

Within the communal context, the chances that factors believed inappropriate to decisions will instead influence them are tremendously increased. With few exceptions here, roles are vaguely defined and narrowly recognized; most are not geared to a system of tangible rewards, and few restraints operate against irresponsibility. The number of latent identities available is vastly increased, and any decision is interpretable within a wide range of perspectives. Because it is easy to assume that actions are based upon motives and interests other than those manifestly relevant, suspicion is natural and the tissue of public confidence thin and fragile.

From the negative standpoint, it is clear from what has just been said that episodes not identified with the public interest will tend to be defined as instances of one or another "selfish interest" exploiting the public. The chances of additional constructive effort, after such definitions, are not great. Probably the most effective step to limit to manageable proportions conflict among numerous special interests relevant to the communal context is to identify development action goals with the common good.

On the positive side, we would stress the great power and momentum that attach to things clearly in the public interest. As Sower has noted, there is evidence to indicate that "senti-

10. See James Coleman, *Community Conflict*, 25–26.

11. See Alvin Gouldner, "Organizational Analysis," in Robert K. Merton, Leonard Broom, and Leonard S. Cottrell, Jr., eds., *Sociology Today, Problems and Prospects* (New York: Basic Books, Inc., Publishers, 1959), 400–428.

ments about the total community" are more powerful forces "than the special interests of individuals or groups."[12] The "fund of good will"[13] latent in every locality would seem to be the ultimate source of power for community development. Without tapping this, little chance appears to exist for anything more than a succession of emergency efforts, launched under crisis conditions. A continuity of planned improvement efforts seems virtually impossible if the contribution to the public good cannot be reasonably demonstrated.

We have already noted certain conditions in the situation that inhibit the linkage of action episode goals to the public good. What factors or forces are there that make the effort feasible? Beyond the opportunities provided by emergencies or crises, which are certainly not inconsiderable, the major sources of leverage are three. The first is the utilization of that consciousness of the common good manifest in the mutual awareness of a number of persons of their commonly threatened private interests.[14] When people in neighborhoods organize to protect private property values endangered by some proposed change, or when some other movement is thus generated, not only does a clear linkage to a publicly defined common good become available, but other comparable efforts of collective significance may also identify with this newly salient element of the general welfare.

The second source of leverage is the use of surveys or research—a careful and thorough collection and exposition of relevant facts. Both the skill and specialization demanded for

12. Christopher Sower, "The State of Knowledge About the Roles of 'Knowledge Center Development Organizations' in Achieving the Goals of Development Planning" (East Lansing: Michigan State University, January, 1963, 8. Mimeographed).

13. See Christopher Sower, "Working Papers: The Roles of Organizations in Achieving National Development Goals—The Case of Ceylon," papers prepared while serving as a member of a United Nations Technical Mission to Ceylon, December, 1961, to March, 1962, pp. 111–18 and Appendix A–2. (Mimeographed.) Also see Sower, "The State of Knowledge."

14. I am indebted to my colleague Dr. John B. Stephenson for the idea that the common good is often generated from threatened private interests.

such an operation and the detachment necessary to minimize potential charges of bias may require that such procedures be linked to the third source of leverage. This involves the use of personnel and organizational resources from administrative echelons beyond the locality. Special information, guidelines, loans, and grants-in-aid from state, regional, or national sources, private and public, can aid immensely in establishing the claim that the goals and operation of a program are in the public interest. Outside speakers or consultants with expertise and prestige may be especially helpful in validating this connection.

The relationship here is very complex. We should not imply that whatever is recommended by the prestigious "outsider" will or should be accepted by locality representatives or that local values can always serve as the measure of what will contribute to long-range betterment. It may be difficult at times to make effective use of "outsiders." In some cases they may be restricted to legitimizing, with their additional prestige, what the local leaders already have decided, and this may not square with the requirements for long-range development. Local values are not always congruent with realistic development programs; Adrian has pointed out that the strength of accepted folk wisdom may constitute a major force inhibiting such programs.[15] Indeed, if local values are widely divergent from realistic program requirements, long-range development may require that the community development worker admit that action for improvement is impossible at one or another time. In some instances, the worker must await a more auspicious time for the particular skills and approach he can offer.

In essence, effective community development involves both a realistic assessment of the requirements of the common good and a hard evaluation of the degree to which consistency with the society's values can be demonstrated within action episodes. Seldom is such consistency or inconsistency demonstrable in advance. In nearly all instances, some aspects of an action effort will be strongly supported by, others will appear

15. Charles R. Adrian, "The Folklore of Community Development," *Adult Leadership*, 11, No. 10 (April, 1963).

quite inconsistent with, and still others may seem almost independent of, any salient value commitments. Indeed, more often than not, the relationship between action episode goals and societal values within the relatively fluid situation of a communal context will depend more upon the unfolding of events and group and personal relationships than upon inherent logic.

THE SOCIAL COMPONENT

The analysis of the pattern of persons and groups operating within and among action episodes constitutes the heart of those implications of community development we might label sociological. The importance of this pattern is difficult to overemphasize. If actual practice is to consist of the best that is known, sophisticated social organization would be a requirement in the realm of creative efforts. Yet, as the Blacks have so well stated, acknowledging the gap between knowledge and practice projects confusing individualistic explanations about this inherently social problem.

> This gap is frequently accounted for by such overly simple statements as "people are that way," "that's human nature," "there are no leaders in our community," and "man is irrational." Our thinking, on the contrary, is that the spotlight should be refocused from the individual and his irrationality to group processes and social machinery. Rational men working as individuals without social machinery cannot solve some kinds of community problems. Men as they are, with both rational and irrational tendencies, can achieve considerable success in problem solving if they have effective social machinery.[16]

Development effort continuity requires the establishment and maintenance of social machinery continuously adapted to the changing dimensions of two basic problems. These problems are the institution of a social organization indigenously recognized as legitimate and representative of a particular residential society, and the maintenance of constructive rela-

---

16. Therel R. Black and Jerrilyn Black, *Community Problems and Group Participation*, Agr. Exp. Sta. Bull. 411 (Logan, Utah: Utah State University, March, 1959), 17.

tionships between this organization and agents representing various other administrative echelons.

The difficulties of achieving an action organization incorporating groups with legitimate interests in a constantly changing community context are great indeed. As times change, perceptions of the components of collective interest and the definitions of the communal context must and do undergo change. What was of little consequence to a population in the past may demand careful attention today—witness the emerging struggles over air pollution and open housing. From issue to issue or celebration to celebration, units having direct interests in collective processes vary, and this variation constitutes a major obstacle to the establishment or continuance of a legitimately representative body. If the constituency of this body is to remain in reasonably close alignment with the realities of legitimate interests, frequent adjustments are necessary.

The difficulties come not only from shifts in relevance due to social change or to the differential impact of diverse issues; they flow also from the fact that parties with special interests in the outcome of communal issues are, for the most part, groups with primary allegiances to entities other than the resident collectivity. As occupational specialization and urban growth have increased and as other parts of what Warren refers to as the "great change"[17] have unfolded, formal organizations have geared the energies of larger numbers of people around special goals of education, economic production, health maintenance, welfare servicing, and religious functioning. The corporations, institutions, and agencies operating within these sectors of life realize their needs and requirements and retain employees with clear responsibilities to state, document, and fight for these interests.

THREE OBSTACLES TO COMMUNITY MATURITY. The community has little comparable formal structure by which to secure for its ends the primary allegiances of individuals and groups. As a group in formation, the community has at least three basic obstacles to overcome in its efforts to gain relative maturity.

17. Roland Warren, *The Community in America*, 53–94.

The community must first compete for time, energy, and resources with established structures already possessing highly developed systems of reward and punishment. Kemper has made the significance of this explicit in a recent analysis of deviant behavior.[18] He notes that within a hierarchical structure, every incumbent of a position of authority represents the establishment to those below him. The person in high position within a formal organization is expected to act for and in the interest of the organization. He does so by idealizing the offerings and promises of the organization and by stressing to the members their obligations to the organization. To a considerable degree, the effectiveness of this process depends upon the rewards and punishments available to him by virtue of his authoritative position within the organization.

The second obstacle to the community's maturing as an operating group is the ideology of distrust with which we, at least in the United States, tend to surround the position of politician. Generally speaking, his is the chief role in the meager "table of organization" of the resident population collectivity. As natural as this tendency to suspicion may be within the value context noted above, by depriving its major role incumbent of the public support needed to validate his actions in the public interest, it further weakens the already inadequate social structure of the community.

The third obstacle has to do again with the character of the context for which a legitimately representative social organization is sought. One prerequisite to any such organization is specification of the basis on which authority is delegated by the group to certain role incumbents. Thompson and Bates[19] have pointed out that where activities are relatively routine and output standards are reasonably specific—as within a factory—authority is easily handled. But where such is not the case, as in a hospital or a university, the definition and maintenance of authority is much more difficult. In these cases, where it rests

18. Theodore D. Kemper, "Representative Roles and the Legitimation of Deviance," *Social Problems*, 13 (Winter, 1966), 288–98.

19. James D. Thompson and Frederick L. Bates, "Technology, Organization, and Administration," *Administrative Science Quarterly*, 2 (December, 1957), 325–43.

so much upon agreement and consensus, authority enforcement confronts continual measurement, validation, and ethical problems.

Here again the communal context exhibits difficulties of an extreme nature. Little indeed is routine, and the outcomes of effort are so variously significant to so many that the bases of legitimate authority are particularly difficult to clarify and stabilize. As a result of this relative vacuum of specified authority, collective policy has succeeded almost accidentally in an "ecology of games"— banking, education, newspapering, etc.[20] Each organization or "game" has tended to use the communal context for its own purposes; with such inadequate organizational resources at its command, the surprising fact is not how little of the collective interest gets results, but how much.

In general, a continuing legitimation of representation from all the major interest sectors in the community must be the objective. To spell out the details this objective would involve in different circumstances is beyond our current scope, but we may suggest the gross types of social units that must be represented to avoid major interruptions in development continuity.

Three main types of interest constitute points of relatively constant reference in the process of planning and executing action episodes. The first focus of interest is geographic locale. Depending upon the substance of the particular action episode, one or another geographic area or region of a local society may become particularly significant to the collective enterprise. Over the span of a series of action episodes, however, development continuity would seem most secure when all geographic segments of the locality are represented among the episodes' active participants. This is no way precludes the importance of episodes where the main geographic unit represented is the total area, but action episodes must often be evaluated for relevance to those demands that stem from the special or unique interests of one or another neighborhood.

The second interest component demands frequent checks of the pertinence that action programs have for various institu-

20. Norton Long, "The Community as an Ecology of Games," *American Journal of Sociology,* 64 (November, 1958), 251–61.

tional sectors,[21] as well as care to see that all action episodes are not oriented just to education, health, etc. Nevertheless, certain episodes of great importance may be relevant either in ways entirely exclusive of institutional considerations or in ways that combine several of them. Continuity seems to rest, in part, upon the inclusion of action episodes geared to all such patterns of relevance.

The third type of interest has to do with the balance between lay or political influence on the one hand, and technical or specialized influence on the other. Continuity in development action sustains itself when the list of recognized action episode participants contains both those who have a political following—whose source of influence rests upon the popularity they command—and those who have a technical or professional speciality—whose source of influence derives from their validated knowledge or technical skill. Technical competence and political astuteness are both indispensable to development system continuity.

RELATIONSHIPS BETWEEN THE LOCALITY SYSTEM AND THE OUTSIDE WORLD. Competence rests upon both training and resources and, since the sources of these are from the expansion of knowledge and capital in the scientific world, we must face the problem of forging constructive relationships between the locality system and the outside world—the second of the major set of difficulties confronting the development worker within the social component.

Learning to combine relevant parts of programs from different echelons is a must in today's world of specialization and intricate symbiotic interdependencies. Few extra-local resources were needed for a house-raising among pioneer neighbors. But a self-help housing program for low-income families today requires not only a cooperative group of low-income families but also a "sponsoring organization to provide funds and technical

21. Sutton has given some preliminary data showing that the distribution of community activities among different institutional sectors probably varies among different localities. See Willis A. Sutton, Jr., "Toward a Universe of Community Actions," *Sociological Inquiry*, 34 (Winter, 1964), 48–59.

supervision; suitable sites or existing structures that can be remodeled; a source of long-range mortgage money or out-right grants to cover cost of materials and land; and technical assistants who understand management procedures, and building codes."[22]

Suppose the problem is developing industry: Effective techniques now demand that a wide array of "outside" talent and resources be geared to the ideas and interests of a number of local persons. The terms of a proposal recently submitted for funding to the federal government to stimulate grass-root industrial development in ten Appalachian towns illustrate the extensive interrelations. Part of the plan stipulated "special technical teams to work with communities"; "local funds and federal or state loans with technical assistance and management talent" and "experts in the fields of management, finance, marketing, production and manpower training."[23]

Few would deny that outside support is a requisite to continuity of effort by any residential population, yet we frequently fail in our efforts to establish working relationships among these different organizational levels.[24] Doing so involves establishing relationships among personnel representing groups with widely varying goals and bases of authority. In this process, the tendency to form barriers around emergent in-group and out-group conceptions is a persistent source of difficulty. To highlight the generic character of these social factors, we shall direct our discussion in terms of an oversimplified situation comprehending only one intra-extra group dimension. We will thus think of representatives of the local community as "insiders" or the "in-group," and those speaking for groups from any or all echelons beyond the locality as "outsiders" or the "out-group."

22. See "Self-Help Housing Plan Proposed for Appalachia," *Louisville Courier-Journal* (February 3, 1967), 1–B.

23. See "U.S. Asked to Help Appalachia Grow Own Industries," *Louisville Courier-Journal* (February 3, 1967), 1–B.

24. Evidence of this is available almost daily in the press. "Creative federalism" is only one of the numerous indications before us that there is a rapidly growing demand that methods be developed to improve the meshing of goals, activities, and timing of people working at different echelons of administration.

When insiders seek outside aid, they are often unrealistic in their approach. Plans may be so far along that the outsider in effect adds no more to them than the prestige of his "expert" approval. The right of outside groups to function in the locality may meet public challenge, and their programs or personnel face competitors in an unfavorable light. These actions and the way insiders make their requests and defend their prerogatives severely undermine the structure of support for the very outside programs they need.

On the other hand, the outsiders' failure to grasp the social realities they confront is just as marked. Their faith in the efficacy of each new special program seems almost unlimited. They may say their success depends upon the way their programs operate in the field, but this is seldom operationalized realistically by careful integration with the work already going on to which it is related and upon which much of its success inevitably depends. By and large, the outsider treats the locality as a means to his own ends. As Sower has noted, "Throughout human history the residents of the locality appear to have been perceived by outsiders as primarily inefficient and subject to manipulation, not education."[25]

The absence of systematic channels of communication between them is a manifestation of the ignorance each party in the development process has of his need of the other. Only with an organized effort can each party contribute his resources and ideas to needed collaboration. Yet seldom does sufficient man-hour support for two-way communication between these echelons build into development planning. To urge workers in action episodes to be sensitive to the opportunities offered by other programs and to be aware of the effects their actions have upon others is not enough. A minimum requirement is the institutionalization of communicator roles within both the intra- and extra-local systems. Specific persons must be responsible for analyzing the factors affecting inside-outside relationships and for executing the contacts required to operate the two-way flow of communication essential to constructive relationships.

25. Christopher Sower, "External Organizations and the Locality." Mimeographed paper presented before the meeting of the American Sociological Association, 1959, 7.

Nonetheless, this is only a start. If any extended continuity of development is to be achieved, more is demanded than the assignment of responsibilities for inside-outside communication. A major reorientation must take place. Realism dictates that development planning be grounded at least in part on the needs different echelons of operations have for each other.[26] Let us consider the social structures and procedures that will help make these assumptions regularly operational in our work.

If social organization to sustain mutually advantageous inside-outside relationships is to occur, it is the outsiders who must assume the main initiative and responsibility. It is they who have the resources required for the job—the access to knowledge and experience and the strength of administrative sanctions needed for implementation.

An effective arrangement must combine two closely related phases. Communication and some operational coordination must be instituted first among those major programs functioning within localities, but with authority and resource anchorages outside them at a level "above" the locality. Agencies or organizations of various types must be among these communication and coordination structures, since communal action episodes may involve almost any facet of collective life. A number of these extra-local coordinating efforts of one type or another are now emerging,[27] documenting the fact that community development does involve activity and organization at levels beyond as well as within the locality.

The second aspect of this effort to be initiated by outsiders is the establishment of procedures by which information and

26. T. R. Batten has put it this way: "Most agencies are genuine in their desire to help people and most people are willing to accept help if it comes in acceptable form." T. R. Batten, "Interaction Between National Agencies and Local Groups," *Autonomous Groups* (Autumn, 1959–Winter, 1960), 11–13.

27. An example is the Kentucky Development Committee. This is a voluntary group of some 40 agencies, offices, and organizations, each of which is seeking on a more-than-local, frequently state-wide, basis to foster either general or specialized development (in health, education, industry, agriculture, family welfare, recreation, etc.) in the local communities of Kentucky.

explanation important for various development operations will transmit "up" and "down" between the local and extra-local echelons of development functioning. Every extra-local development organization—be it a utilities company, the Girl Scouts, the cooperative extension service, a welfare council, or chamber of commerce—has its own procedures for sending and receiving messages and otherwise integrating local and extra-local offices within its organization. We are only suggesting that comparable arrangements for inside-outside transmissions and integrations among communal units are necessary to development action continuity.

But, while outside initiative seems necessary to establish the social framework for effective operations, the execution of these operations demands careful consideration of both local and extra-local interests. Each must be allowed the room it needs to exercise its particular kind of competence. In general, locality insiders have the right, within democratic principles and procedures, to decide what they want to do, what program opportunities and other outside aids they wish to accept, and how they will organize. On the other hand, outsiders would seem to have the right, within stipulations of objective knowledge and professional criteria, to decide what local entities and programs they will support and what the basic terms of their aid will be. Each has an obligation to communicate to the other the information and rationale he has that the other needs to arrive at an informed decision on matters of mutual concern.

Continuity of action seems to demand that a considerable measure of genuine choice be left to each side. In spite of enlarged bureaucracies and obvious tendencies toward centralized control, this does seem possible in the development process. Just as the "enabling principle" has greatly extended the alternatives available to local communities,[28] improved inside-outside consultations throughout the course of action episodes may increase the realistic prerogatives open to extra-local agencies. Within a democratic order, mutually beneficial en-

28. See Robert C. Stone, "Factors in the Interaction of Community and Nation." Abstracts of papers presented before the meeting of the American Sociological Association, 1961.

largements of autonomy may be basic to viable development systems.

THE TEMPORAL COMPONENT

Timing is a critical factor in community action. To a large extent an understanding of action dynamics is dependent upon the grasp we can achieve of temporal structure of action episodes. This involves not just time per se, but the order of events —their sequential, concurrent, and rhythmic character—and the durations of the episode's total span and of the stages comprising its significant subparts. We must also consider the temporal factors involved in the conflux of a number of action episodes in the same communal context.

Little is known about the temporal pattern of the sets of communal action episodes that together constitute the collective life of a resident population, yet the significance of such patterns to planned development activity could hardly be questioned. The dimensions of these patterns are definable by the total number of communal action episodes and their distributions among temporal types, according to rhythm of occurrence and extent of duration. During the course of a year, about 120 community action episodes were found in one town of about 120,000 and about 45 in each of two smaller ones of about 5,000 population. Although not all these were in effect throughout the entire year, about 70 were going on at any one time in the large town and between 20 and 30 in each of the smaller places.[29]

Not all episodes are of the same rhythmic character. Some special ones, like building a water system or holding a referendum, take place infrequently and irregularly. Cyclical episodes, like fund drives or Founder's Day pageants, come about at regular intervals once or twice a year. Others, like operating a clothing bank, are continuous—active to some degree throughout the entire year. At any one time, some 15 special action epi-

29. Willis A. Sutton, Jr., "Community Actions and Action Patterns in Three Kentucky Towns." Mimeographed paper read before the meeting of the Southern Sociological Society, 1964.

sodes and from three to seven episodes of a cyclical or continuous type occurred in towns of 5,000, while in the larger place
these rates were about double.[30] While few residents are aware
of all these episodes and fewer still are active in any significant
proportions of them, the sizable number of different types that
coexist at any one time suggests that temporal juxtaposition
may be an influential factor in action dynamics.

Duration is also important. Most special community action
episodes identified in the above three places lasted more than a
year, and almost a third of them stretched over periods longer
than three years. In addition, almost two-thirds of the "cyclical" episodes observed lasted three months or longer each
year.[31] Clearly, the accomplishment of community action episodes requires extended periods of time. One reason for this
requirement is the slow rate at which events unfold. The over-
all rate for nine special community action episodes, which
lasted an average of 39 months, was only one event per week.[32]

This slow pace and the consequent extended duration of
community actions result from the conditions that surround
action in the communal context. Because the limits that define
who and what may be relevant for such actions are fluid and
diffuse, widening or narrowing in accordance with the diverse
agenda before the collectivity, and because the number of people and groups with legitimate concerns about public questions
is large in any event, there are always substantial obstacles to
overcome in the process of collective action. Added to all this
is the need to fit program options and special interests from the
outside into the network of indigenous goals and activities.

Under these conditions action in each case depends upon the
build-up or confluence of a relatively unique set of forces that,
in large part, is an emergent not easy to anticipate. Here the
parties in a social interchange have to compile as they go the
information needed to define the rewards and costs attendant

30. Sutton, "Community Actions."
31. Sutton, "Community Actions."
32. Willis A. Sutton, Jr., "The Socio-Temporal Structure of Community
Activities." Mimeographed paper read before the meeting of the Society
for the Study of Social Problems, 1964.

upon supporting a particular goal. Thompson has termed this aspect in any course of interaction the "sounding out" process.[33] When numerous persons and groups hold pieces of the total information needed to form a plan and the sections of authority necessary to secure commitments to action, the time required for this process is extensive.

Since the early stages of community action episodes inevitably involve much uncertainty, every interested party must keep commitments minimal while seeking maximum information. This is one reason it is difficult to get action efforts started. The contingencies involved are so complex that it is virtually impossible to assess the consequences of any line of movement.[34]

These conditions not only explain why community action episodes take so long, but they also help clarify the special importance the early stages of episodes have for their ultimate outcomes. The decisions and directions within these stages largely determine which parties will exert major and which minor influence upon questions at issue. As Sower has said,

> The way in which the initiation process [is] first organized and the project first presented to the public, is an important variable in predicting the acceptance, neutrality, or opposition of different segments of the "relevant order" . . . and in predicting whether the project ever . . . [will be] successful. . . . If the initiation process [is] perceived as "captured" by one segment of the community for its own benefit, . . . then legitimate bases . . . [are] laid for the development of the opposition to the project.[35]

Detailed analysis is a requirement for all subsequent stages

33. James D. Thompson, "Organizations and Output Transactions," *American Journal of Sociology*, 68 (November, 1962), 309–24.

34. For further development of this theme, see Jessie Bernard, "Social Problems as Problems of Decision," *Social Problems*, 6 (Winter, 1958–1959), 212–21.

35. Christopher Sower, "Working Papers: The Roles of Organization in Achieving National Development Goals: The Case of Ceylon." Papers prepared while author was serving as member of a United Nations Technical Assistance Mission to Ceylon, December, 1961—March, 1962. Appendix A–3. (Mimeographed.)

and for the interrelations among them; timing is crucial throughout. Acknowledging agreement upon goals, assigning responsibilities, injecting facts, funds, or other resources into the situation—each and all may be of little value unless they are brought about at appropriate points within the meaningful flow of events. Yet we can say little, in principle, about the meaning of "appropriate," or about how specifically temporal variation affects action outcomes. This is because we have yet to develop a conceptual scheme for classifying the flow or process aspects of complex social activity that are adaptable both to the realities of streams of events in the natural world and to the theoretical dimensions necessary for the comparison of seemingly disparate episodes. Some conceptualizations of action stages have been constructed,[36] and a few related empirical analyses carried out,[37] but we cannot state the generalized forms of sequential patterns or the conditions under which one or another of these will precipitate successful or unsuccessful action.

IMPLICATIONS OF THE PACE OF ACTION EPISODES. Certain implications for development continuity can be specified from the slow

36. For examples of this work, see: George M. Beal and others, *Social Action and Interaction in Program Planning* (Ames: The Iowa State University Press, 1966), particularly 74–89; Roland Warren, *The Community in America*, 315–20; Christopher Sower and others, *Community Involvement*; Murray G. Ross, *Community Organization, Theory and Principles* (New York: Harper and Brothers, 1955), 132–52; Harold F. Kaufman, "Toward an Interactional Conception of Community," *Social Forces*, 38 (October, 1959), 8–17; Paul A. Miller, *Community Health Action, A Study of Community Contrast* (East Lansing: Michigan State College Press, 1953), 13.

37. For example, see: George M. Beal and others, *Social Action*; Christopher Sower and others, *Community Involvement*; Miller, *Community Health Action*; John Holik and V. Wayne Lane, "A Community Development Contest as a Catalytic Agent in Social Action," *Rural Sociology*, 26, No. 2 (June, 1961), 157–69; George Beal and others, *Social Action in Civil Defense, The Strategy of Public Involvement in a County Civil Defense Educational Program*, Rural Sociology Report No. 34, Iowa Agr. and Home Economics Exp. Sta. (Ames: Iowa State University, 1964); and Willis A. Sutton, Jr., "Socio-Temporal Structure."

pace and extended duration typical of communal action episodes. These temporal characteristics pose serious difficulties for development workers. The process of collective effort lasts so long and moves so slowly that even citizens interested in communal affairs have difficulty following them. By the time a goal that was set two or three years earlier is achieved, the character of the accomplishment is so attenuated that little satisfaction accrues from the achievement. The boost to identity and pride that is the usual accompaniment of accomplishment, whether individual or collective, is almost entirely lost.

From this it seems clear that workers seeking to facilitate the community development process must find ways of doing two things basic to, though certainly not guarantors of, collective action continuity. They must first find and improve techniques by which the essentials of previous actions may be quickly reviewed and made relevant for successively emerging phases of extended episodes. The role needed may be analogous to that of the personal secretary. Not only would the community development worker maintain a calendar[38] and other significant records for the community, but he would also provide up-to-date briefings to help orient it to unfolding situations.

Development workers must undertake a second job that seems dictated by these temporal characteristics—that of promoting more realistic attitudes toward the temporal requirements of collective actions. Empirical research to document the character of realistic temporal standards is greatly needed, but more may be done to explain why community actions require so much time for their accomplishment. When the reasons are more widely understood, feelings of collective frustration and defeat may be considerably reduced.

Conclusion

We have taken complex action episodes as the units generic for understanding community development and have organ-

38. A community calendar has long been an established aid for development workers, but additional techniques are needed not only for systematizing community records but also for keeping them readily available.

ized our analysis in terms of the three components—value-goal, social, and temporal—whose characteristics and interrelations constitute the basic structure of such streams of action. The focus of our analysis has been on communal episodes—those largely deliberate efforts of place-related resident populations to meet their collective policy and identity problems. Holding the epitome of community development to be such guidance of these activities that collective effectiveness becomes cumulative, we have sought to identify and analyze the social factors confronting the development worker trying to foster such action continuities.

Much of our analysis suggests that community development rests ultimately upon our ability to meld within one operation two quite different sets of social forces. The first is the power of group cohesion and *esprit de corps*; the second is the strength derived from the accumulated capital of mankind, whether of finances, knowledge, or know-how.[39]

Combining these forces in community development faces the worker with two related but somewhat different tasks. In reference to group cohesion and pride, the task is one of stimulating and nurturing the growth of identity and *esprit* for a resident population unit. In the face of strong loyalties already committed to other social entities and in the midst of today's increasing rates of geographic mobility, one might question whether these relatively amorphous entities we have termed place-related populations can be brought to manifest any significant degree of group identity and pride.

Activities and people are geared together, however crudely, at numbers of levels by reason of residential scope. Collectivities form, re-form, and exhibit different degrees of group morale. We know something of the reason for this variation. The pride and belonging characteristic of a group are a product of the experiences people have in working together on things they themselves define as rewarding for their collective interests.

39. I am indebted to Dr. Carl C. Taylor for this general concept of community development as a method by which human knowledge and capital might be joined to group *esprit*. Taylor developed this concept in a similar fashion in a lecture at the University of Kentucky in 1958.

The starting point has its origin in the needs of some significant part of a collectivity.[40] These needs are fundamental to the community development process.[41]

This is not to say that any and all representations of such needs are to be treated as equivalent or accepted at face value as bases for realistic development work.[42] It is rather to emphasize that pride and cohesiveness will come to serve as an actual, rather than merely a potential, power source for community development only when locality members themselves recognize episode goals as contributing to their own common good, and only when those who carry the episode forward do so as the recognized representatives of the residential collectivity.

The task that the community developer faces with reference to utilizing humanity's general capital fund is getting sufficient coordination in the application of highly specialized resources so that the specific needs of specific places at particular times may generally meet adequate and appropriate resources.

This problem must be attacked at each of a number of echelons, but it is only through some system of information

40. This may require some clarification. By using the word *people* we do not mean to refer to every resident or even to a majority of a place-related population even within such a unit as a village of only 40 families. We would fully agree that if all or a majority of the people in such a unit were required to participate before population cohesiveness could be used, we would never be able to attribute group pride or cohesiveness to a resident population unit. By *people* and by *significant portion*, we refer to any certain residents in their roles as residents and to others acting as representatives of residents who work together in behalf of the residential collectivity. They may constitute either a very large or only a tiny proportion of the total population, but when they act in behalf of such a unit's collective interests and are perceived by the population as a part of their legitimate representatives, we are justified in contending that a locality-based unit capable of identity and of social cohesiveness is real.

41. It is because of this fact that community development cannot be tied primarily to any one focus of interest, whether health, industry, agricultural productivity, education, or any other. To remain viable, the process must stay adaptable to the real demands of these indigenously perceived needs and interests.

42. We cannot go into the issues and techniques that this aspect of community development procedure involves. Suffice to say that it is at the procedural point where there is one of the greatest needs for careful specialized help.

exchange and coordination at levels above the locality that outside influences, so often today competitive and conflictive in their options and demands, can be brought to serve locality structures and their development efforts, rather than to disrupt them.

From the sociological perspective, community development may be viewed as an emergent effort to provide the social structuring needed by geographically based population units to enable them to engage in the relatively efficient decision-making that, up to now, has seemed applicable only to special-purpose social organizations. From the intricate elaborations of the spatial and temporal responsibilities developed for persons and groups in these latter type enterprises has come enormous productivity in goods and special services. The ultimate promise of community development may be an ability to build similar structures by which the civic energies of place-related population units may be released for the more rapid enlargement of the common good.[43]

While our knowledge and theory do not yet meet the challenge, such a social achievement is not an idle dream. Without knowing exactly how, we have occasionally, for a little while, fashioned the social instruments adequate to the task.

43. That new levels of social structuring do occur was expressed in the following way by Homans: "Society does not just survive; in surviving it creates conditions that, under favorable circumstances, allow it to survive at a new level. Given half a chance, it pulls itself up by its own bootstraps. How can we account in any other way for the emergence of a civilization from a tribe?" See George C. Homans, *The Human Group* (New York: Harcourt, Brace & Co., 1950), 272.

CHAPTER 4

The Psychological Implications
of the Community Development Process

W A R R E N C. H A G G S T R O M

A social system (a family, a work organization, a community, a society, etc.) consists of two dissimilar components. One component is visible: a set of bodies that move in patterns exhibiting mutual interrelationships; the other component is invisible: a symbolic control system that establishes and regulates those movements of member bodies stemming from participation in the social system in question.[1] An adding machine illustrates the differences in a simple fashion. On the one hand is the visible component: a set of parts moving in a pattern that exhibits the relationships among them; on the other hand is the invisible component: the set of numbers and the operation of addition that together determine the kinds of movements that occur among the parts.

But here we face a problem. What an adding machine does depends only partly on the system that has been built into it; it also depends on the particular numbers an operator has selected to be added. We can say, therefore, that part of the symbolic control system of an adding machine is internalized, built into it, while another part is situational and varies from time to time. Similarly, what a social system does depends partly on the symbolic control system that has been built into it and partly on additions from the situation of the social system in question.[2]

1. For discussions of the invisible component of social systems, see Peter Berger and Thomas Luckmann, *The Social Construction of Reality* (Garden City: Doubleday & Company, Inc., 1966), and the *Collected Papers of Alfred Schutz* (The Hague, Netherlands: Nijhof, 1962, 1964, 1966).

2. Discussions of the machine as symbolic system include Norbert Wiener's classical *Cybernetics* (New York: John Wiley & Sons, Inc., 1949), and W. Ross Ashby's *Design for a Brain*, 2d ed. (New York: John Wiley & Sons, Inc., 1960).

The analogy will carry us no further. The symbolic control system of a social system is much more complex and imprecise. It can sometimes create the situation to which it then responds, and it competes with other symbolic control systems for the opportunity to regulate its bodies. The symbolic control system of a social system may not be explicitly known to any of its members, although they are all acquainted with some part of it.

Since communities are social systems, community development also has a visible and an invisible component. The latter may be taken as development of the collective psychology of the community, development of the symbolic system by which a community regulates its members. This chapter will describe the collective psychology of the community development process.

The following paragraphs begin with a description of the collective psychology of a community: the symbolic fabric of enduring groups and its extension over a territory to form a community. We then consider two major kinds of community development: the creation of organizations of marginal people through which marginal people can enter the majority community; and the internal development of community subsystems.

THE SYMBOLIC FABRIC

Let us begin with a consideration of enduring groups, as distinguished from transitory assemblages of people. An enduring group may be composed of people who live on the same block, work in the same office, meet together because of a common interest, or simply the members of a family.[3]

3. For illustrations of enduring groups, see Charles Horton Cooley, "Primary Groups," in *Social Organization* (Glencoe, Ill.: The Free Press, 1965), Chap. 3; *The Family*, Norman W. Bell and Ezra Vogel, eds. (Glencoe, Ill.: The Free Press, 1960); Ruth Jaffe, "Group Activity as a Defense Method in Concentration Camps," *Israel Annals of Psychiatry and Related Disciplines*, 1, 2 (October, 1963), 235–43; and J. R. Fox, "Therapeutic Rituals and Social Structure in Cochiti Pueblo," *Human Relations*, 13 (1960), 291–303. Most of the literature concerning *small* groups does *not* fall into this category as, for example, most studies reported in *Small Groups*, A. Paul Hare, Edgar F. Borgetta, and Robert F. Bales, eds. (New

An enduring group is affected by some of the objects around it, especially by those objects in its path. The fate of a chess club, for example, may be affected by the prestige and playing strength of another chess club nearby. The enduring group defines and deals with those objects near it that it sees as relevant to it. To continue our illustration, one chess club may define another as a rival, make certain assumptions about the other, and seek to defeat the other in chess tournaments.

Sometimes an enduring group may not see or understand objects near and relevant to it. A chess club may not notice that infirmities of age have affected the playing strength of its members. When the group becomes aware that it has not perceived objects relevant to it, some portion of its situation suddenly appears to be undefined or marginal. Since the enduring group cannot act except on the basis of assumptions concerning the various objects it considers relevant to it, the appearance of marginal or undefined aspects of the situation occurs as a threat. The enduring group makes the necessary assumptions, making the world again subjectively predictable and potentially controllable, even if there is yet little understanding of the object that has suddenly appeared.

Several varieties of elements constitute the process by which the enduring group defines and deals with its situation. There are cognitions—assumptions about the nature of the situation; there are impulses to deal with the situation in one fashion or another; there are ethical rules that guide the course of action of the group along legitimate channels; and there are general principles of science, policy, or ethics, to which appeal may be made to enable the group to select from among alternative courses of action.

The various elements of the symbolic process are related in describable ways to one another in such fashion that a stream of decisions is produced that direct the group along its course of action. Just as with a sentence, any element of the group symbolic process may occur at various times and in various

York: Alfred A. Knopf, Inc., 1955), or Dorwin Cartwright and Alvin Zander's *Group Dynamics: Research and Theory* (Evanston, Ill.: Row, Peterson, 1953).

places. We may refer to each appearance of an element as a *token* of it. Such tokens may be easy or difficult for the group to oppose or to deny. For example, a chess club may find it easy to ignore its rival when the spirit of rivalry is not very strong.

A network of element tokens, each with a series of determinate positions in space and time, constitutes the symbolic fabric that creates and maintains the enduring group and distinguishes it from a collection of people who merely interact regularly.[4]

An enduring group has a symbolic fabric of several layers that reflects various ways in which it defines its situation and determines levels of reality for it; it has a public image, a way in which it presents itself to the world. Different from its public image is its official account of itself, the kind of process that is the basis for minutes made of the meeting of the group. Another level consists of assumptions and beliefs held in common by group members and relevant to action by the group but that, for some reason, are kept from the official account. For example, "everyone knows" gossip about each member in the group, which is taken into account when the group acts, but this gossip does not directly enter into formal group meetings. Or, if members of a group seek to protect each other's feelings, they may disguise the actual bases for what they say when they are in task-oriented discussions. Let us refer to the outcome of this process as unofficial reality. The enduring group primarily defines and deals with official and unofficial reality.

The three layers of the symbolic fabric just mentioned also ensure that there will be other levels of reality. The relevant objects, which the group has not taken seriously, are in the pre-

4. The historical antecedents for this discussion can be found by referring to Chap. 8, "The Preface to the Phenomenology," in Walter Kaufmann's *Hegel* (New York: Doubleday & Company, Inc., 1965), and Part 3, "The Self," in George Herbert Mead's *Mind, Self and Society*, Charles Morris, ed. (Chicago: The University of Chicago Press, 1934). An elaboration of this discussion may be found in Chap. 3, "A Proposed Theory," of my doctoral dissertation, "Self-Esteem and Other Characteristics of Residentially Desegregated Negroes" (University of Michigan, 1962), and in my paper, "Can the Poor Transform the World?", in *Among the People: Encounters With the Poor*, Irwin Deutscher and Elizabeth Thompson, eds. (New York: Basic Books, Inc., Publishers, 1968), Chap. 5.

consciousness of the group. For example, a new high-school chess champion may be recognized as promising, on the basis of knowledge of the games he has played. However, further analysis of his career thus far would have revealed him to have demonstrated an ability to dominate future chess competition in the city. Some objects or thoughts are so threatening to the assumptions on which the group is based that they can appear only in disguised form to the group and must, therefore, remain in the group unconscious.

Further, an enduring group may not be completely in charge of its own symbolic fabric. That is, a group may be identified with another that originates its definitions, as when a social club takes its political views wholesale from a favorite political analyst or when neighborhood factions with widely differing perspectives alternate in control of the definitions held by a block organization.[5]

Depending partly on its ability to mobilize and allocate resources and to acquire and exercise power over its members and its situation, the symbolic fabric of an enduring group contributes to the creation of the reality it defines by determining the meaning and location of objects. That is, the group *decides* whether a quality should be placed in the object or in its beholder. Let us suppose that a member of a discussion group dissents from the prevalent opinion within the group. If his dissent is threatening enough to the group, or unintelligible enough, the group may not admit his opinion into the discussion but, ignoring the content of the dissent, treat it rather as an indication of a personality defect of the dissenter. Or the group may define the dissent as legitimate and concern itself with the truth or falsehood of the dissenting opinion. That is, the group disposes of the opinion in one fashion or in another by deciding that it is inside or outside the realm of discourse.

5. Readings relevant to the preceding paragraphs include Sigmund Freud's famous *Interpretation of Dreams* (New York: Avon Books, 1965); Erving Goffman's *The Presentation of Self in Everyday Life* (Garden City: Doubleday & Company, Inc., 1959); and Daniel Boorstin's *The Image* (New York: Harper and Row, Publishers, 1961). A fascinating, although not erudite, discussion of the Turks as a captive people can be found in H. C. Armstrong's *Gray Wolf* (New York: Capricorn Books, 1933).

Similarly, a community elite may suppose that there is no poverty within the community, and if someone writes a description of existing poverty it will be ignored. If the report is widely publicized, the community elite may ignore its content and define the author of the report and its publicists as trouble-makers and Communists. In so doing, the community elite keeps the report out of its realm of discourse and locates it in an alien, threatening, subversive attack. Since a community elite has considerable power, it is capable of creating its own reality. In this example, the elite may give substance to its need to perceive a poverty-free community by sponsoring an urban renewal project that drives the poor out of the community. The elite can then act as if the poor had never been present. A group does not merely perceive and define; in part it creates social reality, its situation, through the process of perceiving and defining it.[6]

We may say that the symbolic fabric of all groups, taken as a totality, creates and maintains reality, and that without the consensus the symbolic fabric presupposes, one cannot even consider the problem of whether a perception is veridical or distorted.

Often a symbolic fabric weakens and needs repairing or is flimsy and needs strengthening. This can be accomplished if the group secures rewards of central importance for its members. It also may be important to establish barriers to communication, as when some businesses conceal the salaries of executive employees from general knowledge in order to avoid the intraorganizational strains that would otherwise develop. Or, regulated conflict may be used to strengthen the symbolic fab-

6. The great historical progenitor of this view is, of course, Immanuel Kant, *Critique of Pure Reason* (London: Macmillan and Co., Ltd., 1961). The fortunes of Ignac Semmelweis illustrate the point, as related in the fictionalized biography by Morton Thompson, *The Cry and the Covenant* (Garden City: Doubleday & Company, Inc., 1949). In more recent times, illustrations are provided by J. Davidson Ketchum's *Ruhleben* (Toronto: University of Toronto Press, 1965), and Martin Anderson's *The Federal Bulldozer* (Cambridge: The M.I.T. Press, 1964). The previously cited works of Alfred Schutz and of Berger and Luckmann provide a theoretical sociological perspective that is contemporary and consistent with this position.

ric. The wrangling preceding a vote in a union meeting, limited by rules that everyone holds in common, normally strengthens the symbolic fabric of the union.[7]

Finally, the symbolic fabric of enduring groups may contribute to the psychology of members in much the same fashion as does the residue personality members have acquired through childhood socialization.[8] For example, by supporting the status of members, a group also supports their self-esteem. Self-esteem may, alternatively, be a personality trait acquired originally in the bosom of a nurtural family. For most people, the support of an enduring contemporary group is a more certain guarantor of self-esteem than is childhood socialization. As persons fluctuate in status within their groups, their opinions of themselves may also fluctuate, although the origin of fluctuations is likely to be obscured by defenses of members against status anxiety.[9]

Emotion, perception, and motivation are all largely situational, regulated by the symbolic fabric of enduring groups to which people refer.[10] Major psychological changes in people

7. A sociological discussion relevant to this point may be found in Lewis Coser's discussion of realistic conflict in *The Functions of Social Conflict* (Glencoe, Ill.: The Free Press, 1956).

8. By "residue personality," I mean essentially that described by Sigmund Freud and his followers, including as well the attitudes and skills and knowledge acquired in childhood as an enduring set of determinants of behavior.

9. A discussion of literature relevant to this point may be found in Chap. 5 of my doctoral dissertation, "Self-Esteem and Other Characteristics of Residentially Desegregated Negroes."

10. Within the enormous literature concerning the nature of perception, this issue is discussed especially acutely by Jerome S. Bruner, "Social Psychology and Perception," in *Readings in Social Psychology*, Eleanor E. Maccoby, Theodore M. Newcomb, and Eugene L. Hartley, eds. (New York: Henry Holt, 1958), 85–94. There are additional relevant theoretical discussions, including especially pages 1–39 in William Ittelson's *Visual Space Perception* (New York: Springer Publishing Co., Inc., 1960); Fritz Heider's initial three chapters in *Person Perception and Interpersonal Behavior*, Renato Tagiuri and Luigi Petrullo, eds., (Stanford, Calif.: Stanford University Press, 1958); and Ely Devons and Max Gluckman, "Modes and Consequences of Limiting a Field of Study," in *Closed Systems and Open Minds* (Chicago: Aldine Publishing Company, 1964), 158–261.

may follow changes in the symbolic fabric. Depth psychology has two dimensions: One delves into those permanent aspects of the personality that were acquired early in life; the second dimension reaches into the symbolic fabric of enduring groups to which people are oriented. One of the tasks of community development is to learn how to reach the symbolic fabric of enduring groups in order to render psychological aid to persons.

David Riesman has called attention to the increasing "other-directedness" of people in contemporary industrial society.[11] In a rapidly changing society, other-directedness may have a survival value, since it makes people less subject to inappropriate characteristics stemming from the different childhood world. With the situational aspects of personality becoming predominant, concentrating psychological aid in attempts to affect the internalized residue personality would not appear to be the preferred method of treatment.

Enduring groups are related to each other in part through the symbolic fabric that extends between and across them over a territory to form a community. Let us next briefly consider that social entity.

The Community

When people settle in an area and begin to interact with one another, there are common problems and tasks. Children must be nurtured and educated; money must be earned; collective decisions must be made about such matters as the building of roads and the disposal of wastes. From outside the settlement appear both threats and opportunities. The settlement gradually begins to act in response to what it has come to define as its situation.

But not all of the settlement-wide perspectives that emerge are directly related to the action of the community. Gossip finally establishes a consensus about the nature and probable fate of Mrs. Smith's wayward daughter; people believe that it is good luck to hang a horseshoe on the wall of one's house— provided the ends are pointed down so that the Devil cannot

11. David Riesman, *The Lonely Crowd* (New Haven, Conn.: Yale University Press, 1950).

sit in it; common sense may dictate that the cure for a certain kind of skin sore is to have a pregnant woman spit over the victim's shoulder; or people may become preoccupied with the "style" of the current as compared with the former social elite. That is, a set of orientations develops that is generally held by the people of the settlement and enables people and their collectivities to live and act to some extent in a common world in which the objects and concerns in the situation have shared meanings.

The people of the settlement evolve socially patterned feelings, perceptions, orientations, motivations, and modes of action concerning objects and potential objects within and outside the settlement that are most relevant to what it sees as its concerns. The words spoken within the community reflect this process. By now we need no longer speak of it as a settlement: It defines its situation, makes decisions on the basis of part of the definition, and attempts to carry out the decisions—it is now a community.

A community appears in two guises. As an object, it is an interdependent system of neighborhoods, bureaucratic work organizations, interest groups, political parties, and other subsystems, tied together by processes such as transportation, communication, and the circulation of money. The fate of the object community is a function of the separate fates of its subsystems; the symbolic fabric of the object community constitutes the separate symbolic fabrics of its components. In its object guise a community does not act, although it may be an object of action by groups within and around it. Everyone residing within the territorial limits, as well as many who reside elsewhere but who regularly enter, can be said to belong to the object community.[12]

The subsystems in the object community, of course, are not equal. The primary dimension along which subsystems are arranged is power: the extent to which a subsystem is at the mercy of those around it as compared with the extent to which it

12. See Amos Hawley's *Human Ecology: A Theory of Community Structure* (New York: The Ronald Press Company, 1950).

has those about it at its mercy. Some subsystems are very powerful and others very dependent.[13]

In its second guise, the community appears as an acting community, an entity that engages in collective action and embarks on one or more social journeys.[14] To say that a group is part of the acting community is to say that it enters subjectively and objectively into the action process. The group helps to define the community situation, to make decisions on the basis of that definition, or to see to it that community decisions are carried out.

People and groups differentially placed have differential access to the acting community. Most essential are those persons and groups whom one has to see in order to accomplish those things generally regarded as having been done by the community. For example, depending on the community, in order to get a residential area rezoned it may be most useful to see a group within the city council, a number of key business associates, or a political boss with no formal position at all.

Community newspapers play a central role in many acting communities, since they help to establish the common definitions on the basis of which community action can then proceed. At the opposite end of the process, various agencies and businesses that carry out community decisions, from public schools to wrecking companies, can also be regarded as central to the acting community, provided they are influential in the implementation of community decisions.

Most groups that enter the acting community at all enter it only in restricted ways or for temporary periods of time. Race relations and the fine arts may be dominated by women of influential families, while the attraction of new industry may be the preoccupation of civic-minded businessmen and politicians.

13. General discussions include C. Wright Mills, *The Power Elite* (New York: Oxford University Press, Inc., 1956); Gerhard Lenski, *Power and Privilege* (New York: McGraw-Hill, Inc., 1966); and Robert A. Dahl, *Modern Political Analysis* (Englewood Cliffs, N.J.: Prentice-Hall, Inc., 1963).

14. Studies of decision-makers usually concern the acting community, as in Floyd Hunter's *Community Power Structure*, and Robert V. Presthus, *Men at the Top* (New York: Oxford University Press, Inc., 1964).

During a crisis, as when Negroes appear as potential residents in white neighborhoods, a wide range of groups may enter the acting community in order to mobilize it to meet this threat.

PEOPLE OUTSIDE THE ACTING COMMUNITY.   Not all groups seeking to enter the acting community are allowed to do so. For example, the community may boast a society to preserve historical landmarks. But if the community decisions concerning historical landmarks disregard this society and are made solely on the basis of land values and prospective profits, then the society has not been able to enter the acting community. The poor, Negroes, the mentally ill, the mentally retarded, recipients of public welfare, criminals, children, and other entire categories of population are outsiders who seldom enter the acting community.

Although there is a rough correlation between the power of a group in the object community and its centrality in the acting community, these are by no means equivalent. As some studies have indicated, a large corporation may remain outside an acting community while being a powerful component of the corresponding object community. Or a person at the very center of the acting community may have little power in the corresponding object community. He may function, instead, primarily as a broker through whom powerful social forces are expressed in the acting community. If such a broker were to stray from his role of expressing the interplay of community forces he would quickly be replaced.

Community groups that are, and believe they will continue to be, excluded from the acting community tend not fully to identify with it, do not find the community instrumental to the realization of their potentialities, and become alienated from the acting community. In dealing with them the acting community becomes primarily an external force, treating them as objects, as though they were nonhuman objects in the situation external to the acting community. These become marginal groups, held in by the forces of the object community, pushed out by the forces of the acting community. The symbolic fabric of such groups becomes a battleground in which their own perspectives struggle with the alien perspectives of the acting community.[15] Because of its claim to include everyone and every group that seeks inclusion, the acting community cannot recognize in straightforward terms its relationship with the groups it has excluded. This relationship becomes relegated to the collective unconscious of the acting community, which cannot understand the subjective worlds being excluded or even that they are being excluded. That is, the perspectives of those who understand the relationship of marginal groups to the acting community, including socially conscious marginal persons, are unconsciously pushed out of its own awareness by the acting community. The acting community consequently cannot define very accurately this part of its situation, is pathological in dealing with its marginal groups, and finds unanticipated consequences a normal aspect of its program for them.

As groups become marginal they find that the same effort brings less in returns to them. A white middle-class child buys an insider ticket to a life of affluence by his efforts in educational institutions; a Negro lower-class child is not sure what he would buy with the same effort, but it would certainly be less. At best he would end up estranged from his parents, neighborhoods, and friends in a white world in which he has acquired material comforts. At worst he would mow the lawn in the public park for a living. This certainty of less and uncertainty about how much less in turn affects his motivation to struggle for success in someone else's educational institutions. Thus, powerlessness demotivates; the demotivation helps the acting community to stigmatize the increasingly marginal group as inferior; the weight of the stigma again reduces power and motivation. A downward spiral ends with the marginal group powerless and apathetic, getting along as well as it can in its immediate situation, even cooperating, to ease its own

15. Moving discussions of this process can be found in two books by W. E. B. DuBois, *The Souls of Black Folk* (Chicago: A. C. McClurg, 1903), and *Dusk of Dawn* (New York: Harcourt, Brace & Co., 1940). A psychoanalytical account of the outcome has been written by Abram Kardiner and Lionel Ovesey in *The Mark of Oppression* (New York: W. W. Norton & Company, Inc., 1951).

discomfort, in the adoption of the rationale for its plight provided for it by the major community.[16]

Having been moved outside the acting community, marginal groups now appear foreign, mysterious, or menacing to it. Since the subjective perspectives developed within marginal groups are kept outside the consciousness of the acting community, these groups are treated coldly, as though they were resistant to socialization, as outsiders rather than as insiders, with deference to the subjective characteristics naturally taken into account in dealing with fellow insiders. Marginal groups may basically share a single culture and society with the acting community, but, viewed from the social distance of the acting community, their motivations seem incomprehensible.

FAILURE IN COMMUNICATIONS.   For the reasons just mentioned, communication between the acting community and its marginal groups systematically fails. Those groups understand that, by some unknown characteristic of their defining criteria, they have been pushed out, and marginal groups interpret most communications addressed to them from the acting community in terms of this single, overriding fact. But the acting community does not, and cannot, accept this fact, except in a distorted fashion, and must therefore define each exchange of communication with its marginal groups in a way that rationalizes the process for itself.

Negroes, having been excluded from many of the good things of life despite their abilities, are not irrational when they believe that their access to resources will also be irrelevant to ability. Some may then struggle for access to better jobs through political and other forms of legitimate influence and illegitimate manipulation or coercion. For a while the white majority may tolerate their efforts, on the grounds that Negroes have been discriminated against and that the balance must be

16. This has been the fate of the Ainu, an aboriginal race of Japan physically indistinguishable from some varieties of Europeans. For a recent discussion, see John B. Cornell, "Ainu Assimilation and Cultural Extinction: Acculturation Policy in Hokkaido," *Ethnology*, 3, No. 3 (July, 1964), 287–304.

redressed. However, the white majority wants Negroes to become converted into individualistic strivers in a situation in which many Negroes perceive this course of action to be neither possible or desirable. Negro collective action gains the label of illegitimacy; white resentment grows; the white "friends" of Negroes feel slightly betrayed and retire from their advocacy. Finally, Negroes are pushed back again and redefined as incompetent and malicious; they see the forces of discrimination operating with much the same power as ever. The *status quo* has been maintained, with the acting community and the marginal group each convinced that the blame lies with the other.[17]

Even more than the social fabric in general, the community is a site of multiple realities. Each group or person with enough power to impose a definition on its situation may create its own reality and project it into the acting community. The less powerful persons and groups cannot maintain their definitions without becoming sanctioned as illegitimate (criminal or psychotic) and hence becoming trapped in realities created by others. For each of the multiple realities there are meanings that must be excluded as too threatening to entertain and that violate the assumptions on the basis of which the reality was fashioned. Social perception in the sense of perception by groups becomes therefore much more liable to distortion than is perception by persons; the powerless objects near powerful defining groups are likely to become figments of the collective imaginations of their definers. If Negroes are imagined to be inferior, the powerful groups will unconsciously create the conditions that will ensure that Negroes lack the attributes of superiority. A welfare worker may adjust a recipient's budget without fuss, but he would become immediately anxious if he were seriously to entertain the thought that "his" recipients are superior to him or that all men are created equal. Because of the power of organizations, the strategies necessary to ward

17. Most daily newspapers record the majority side of such a struggle. The minority side may be found in such newspapers as *Muhammad Speaks*, such magazines as *Liberator*, and such books as James Baldwin's *The Fire Next Time* (New York: The Dial Press, Inc., 1963), and *The Autobiography of Malcolm X* (New York: Grove Press, Inc., 1965).

off threatening thoughts are simpler than is the case with people and may consist primarily of the mechanisms of denial and rationalization.

The symbolic fabric of a community may be more or less internalized in persons or institutionalized in groups. We may say that it becomes stuck in either personal or social systems, that residues from the past of persons or of social systems remain and help to direct contemporary action processes. Freudian psychology suggested that much of personality stems from childhood; idealistic sociology has suggested an analogous process for social actors. With the impact of technology and the acceleration of the rate of change, the personal and social residues from the past become less helpful to the present. Just as it does not help for a child to become socialized into a view of the world and of social relationships that is far different from the world he will enter as an adult, so it is also disadvantageous for the inheritors of a political party or a professional association to continue carrying the ideological luggage of Marx or Freud. However, it is a practical problem for a contemporary community to reduce the impact of residues from the past without at the same time destroying purpose and direction in the various systems affected. The theoretical solution to this problem is for communities to maintain deeply weighted elements, depth in the symbolic fabric, and a relating of the definition-decision-doing process within its borders to general underlying principles. In this fashion the weight of the past can less often reduce the extent to which people flourish.

Having considered the nature of communities, let us next turn to the community development process itself.

Psychological Implications of the Community Development Process

The nature of communities, standards for the evaluation of communities, and opportunities for intervention all combine to determine the nature of the community development process. Two major varieties of community development have risen from these factors. First in this discussion is the internal development of the acting community or of other subsystems in the object community. Second is the development of the object community through the migration of marginal groups from their original position into the acting community.

A community development specialist may help economic enterprises of government agencies to begin or to become more effective. He may help a village to change in such fashion that its economy is improved or mobilize a neighborhood to attempt self-help housing efforts. These are enterprises that require replacement of portions of the symbolic fabric. For this purpose the community development specialist must intuitively (as with village-level workers) or more analytically understand the symbolic fabric as well as the opportunities available for changing it. He builds on accepted practices and appeals to underlying, collectively held assumptions that can be interpreted or reinterpreted to legitimate the changes he hopes to bring about. He may raise questions about the legitimacy of practices he is attempting to change by applying to them commonly held, underlying assumptions that have not before been applied to them. He may provide the innovations he promotes with an interpretation consistent with the traditions of the population to which he is relating. His *modus operandi* can be found in any text of community development.[18]

INTERNAL DEVELOPMENT OF THE SUBSYSTEMS. The central problem for community development in the United States today lies outside this traditional process. It is the problem of how to achieve further internal development of the complex subsystems of the communities in modern industrial society. Concerning this more urgent problem, there is relatively little knowledge or experience.

Social systems make possible the rationality and morality of people. They provide both the norms in accordance with which truth and value are judged, and also the social reality by reference to which persons can realize the true and the good. On the other hand, social systems are almost always less rational and less moral than are persons.

18. I have found especially useful T. R. Batten's classic *Communities and Their Development.*

The acting community shares the same characteristics. A community fails to detect violations of its housing codes that the children in the vicinity could spot in minutes. It may destroy neighborhoods on behalf of private interests, incarcerate people with deviant views in mental institutions or prisons, maintain a ghetto for Negroes, or covertly promote corruption and crime while overtly attacking both evils. The most backward and cruel acting community is likely to possess the curious perceptual defect that allows it to see itself as being in the vanguard of virtue and progress. More generally, a community normally promotes the mistaken intellectual judgment that equates power with virtue and lack of power with lack of virtue.[19]

In short, social systems tend toward psychosis, and they tend more toward psychosis the more powerful they become. It is not accurate to regard the irrationality of social systems as a reflection of the irrationality of people. Instead, one notices that intellectuals who are competent and stable in their private lives may enter the acting community and provide it with complex rationalizations that support its most monstrous actions. A community may maintain a fantasy of danger from Communists (or other latter-day versions of Satan) within it whether or not such people exist or have any influence. If a person were to exhibit similar symptoms, he would be in danger of being appropriately hospitalized. And, just as important, a community has power that enables it to impose its fantasies and delusions on people. When the acting community embarks on a crusade against communism, any person should be wary of pointing out the absence of any Communists. When the community decides to demolish a low-income neighborhood and replace its housing with luxurious apartment buildings, the people of that neighborhood may be forced to emigrate to other communities, while the luxury apartments remain unoccupied.

The causes for the immorality and stupidity of social systems are apparent. Their power makes it easy for them to maintain perspectives and actions that defy both morality and reality.

19. An analysis of most daily newspapers will illustrate sharply differing treatments of powerful as compared with powerless persons.

The decision processes of social systems tend to be primitive and manipulable by persons and groups in especially favored positions. A powerful social system can employ newspapers, television programs, intellectuals, and public relations firms to rationalize whatever course of action it is embarked upon. Finally, and most important, social systems create social reality by consensual validation and thus create the social situations persons enter and act within. It is as though a paranoid person did not merely believe he was God, but actually possessed the power to draw all those near him into participation in his delusion.

The internal development of the acting community and of other subsystems of such an object community would consist of an incorporation of underlying values, norms for the determination of truth, and rules that orient system actions as much as possible to basic values and truths. In other words, the community development specialist would seek to make such systems more nearly moral and rational and attempt to eliminate the collective psychoses held by social systems within the object community.

Often, however, a community development specialist finds himself in a different role. He is employed by the acting community or one of its subsystems to help rationalize and implement the collective fantasies that have already developed. He becomes an ally of forces that are obstacles to the development of the community he is officially helping to develop and, since social systems control jobs, careers, and resources, it is not easy to see how he can do otherwise. If, as a part of the delusional set of ideas of an acting community, he attempts to work on behalf of rationality and virtue, he is likely at best to find himself ignored and at worst driven out of his career.

How can it become possible for a community development specialist to do what he represents himself as doing with respect to the internal development of such an acting community? One can now only propose possibilities. It may be possible to conduct demonstration research projects on how to increase the rationality and morality of volunteer subsystems—and subsequently use the knowledge gained in intervening in volunteer acting communities. Probably a social movement would have to be developed in each system before it would volunteer for development.

The outcome of such research can only be speculated on at present. It may be that a broadened office of ombudsman[20] could be established in each community, with the responsibility of making public the irrational and immoral aspects of the acting community with which it is associated. The resulting concern could then lead to the employment of community development specialists who would help the community to remedy its defects.

MIGRATION OF MARGINAL GROUPS INTO THE ACTING COMMUNITY. The second variety of community development concerns the migration of marginal groups into the acting community. Marginal groups are concentrated in certain neighborhoods in communities, neighborhoods in which official statistics report a high incidence of poverty, dark skins, mental illness, public assistance—the social characteristics officially defined and treated as evils by the acting community. A community development specialist can help marginal groups by becoming an organizer who helps marginal neighborhoods to create organizations that exercise power, by means of which marginal populations can make the journey into the acting community.

There is reason, however, to question the possibility of such a process. In the United States the odds seem great against successful organizations of marginal populations helping their members to enter powerful, affluent, and domineering acting communities. Marginal neighborhoods are, after all, neighborhoods of a heterogeneous and powerless minority population that has never organized effectively on its own behalf in order to effect social change. In addition, the residents of such neighborhoods are reputed to be inferior in education, intelligence, morality, energy, and responsibility. A high proportion of them are allegedly mentally ill and mentally retarded; the family

20. The office of ombudsman, first created in Sweden, has gained widespread attention throughout the world. It provides for quick and impartial inquiry into citizen complaints of unfair treatment by government. See Walter Gellhorn, *Ombudsman and Others: Citizen's Protectors in Nine Countries* (Cambridge, Mass.: Harvard University Press, 1967).

structure is supposed to have been undermined in many such neighborhoods. The natural approach to marginal people has therefore always been to expect very little of them. Organizations of marginal people have organized, with the help of representatives from the majority community, in order to seek very limited concrete changes, better public welfare benefits, better treatment for children in school, and an increasing sensitivity to marginal people in programs extended by the majority community to help them. That is, attempts to organize marginal neighborhoods have usually been in a context of the presumed inability of marginal populations to effect significant social changes on their own behalf. Helping marginal people has therefore been primarily a process of planning for them.

It is, however, likely that much of the literature about marginal people is of limited value in understanding and evaluating the possibility that they have organizational ability and an opportunity to use it successfully. It is not surprising that marginal people react with apathy to efforts at help that assume their inability and inferiority. The same neighborhoods may have required no outside help in organizing and supporting their churches, sometimes having raised building funds through years of patient effort. The churches do not define their members as inferior but, rather, provide them with the vision of a golden if distant future that can be theirs. On the basis of these and other facts, it is clear that the same population that appears to lack organizational ability and potential in one context demonstrates a considerable amount of such ability and potential in another. We must conclude that it is not a priori impossible for the people of marginal neighborhoods to create their own social action organizations.

STRATEGIES AND TACTICS FOR ENTERING THE ACTING COMMUNITY.
The next question is whether strategies and tactics are possible through which organizations of marginal people can help their members to enter the acting community. In principle, the odds against marginal people succeeding in such an effort are not as great as might be supposed. There are several relevant possibilities.

First, organizations of marginal people can initiate, define, and control the course of conflict with those who stand in the way of their entering the acting community. Such an organization will enter a specific struggle for a limited period of time, on its own terms, to seek specific gains, and break off the conflict at a time and in a manner advantageous to itself.

Suppose the organization discovers that a corporation can, but will not, provide work careers for marginal people. The organization may do nothing with this knowledge until it discovers how the corporation may be vulnerable to an attack for which the organization then prepares itself. The organization may, in such a case, create a consumer boycott of the corporation's products, and have ready specific limited objectives that are projected to result from negotiations with the corporation. During such a struggle, the organization dramatizes its moral integrity and contrasts this with the immorality of a continued policy of exclusion by the corporation. The organization would initiate and control a series of such encounters, over decades if necessary, until small victories added up to major changes.

Second, major changes for marginal people can be accomplished at relatively little cost to the major community. And to admit marginal people into the acting community is already legitimated, since the acting community preaches equality of opportunity for everyone. It is to the self-interest of marginal people to stake everything on their struggle for equality, a struggle that is clearly legitimate; it is to the self-interest of opponents of organizations of marginal people not to devote more than a limited portion of their attention and resources in an illegitimate effort to prevent an outcome that will cost little. The organizations of marginal people can gain in experience and skill more quickly than their opponents, since they are more constantly engaged in struggle. Because of the legitimacy of their cause and their growing power, they are likely to acquire allies. Opponents of organizations of marginal people gradually divide among themselves, and consequently are isolated and beaten.

Third, the major community has a stake in seeing marginal people as inferior. This perception, which allows members of the acting community to continue to see their community as basically good, can be turned into an advantage by organizations of marginal people. In conflicts, their opponents cannot believe that marginal people can have ability and determination, and therefore opponents continually deny or underestimate the superior qualities made evident as marginal neighborhoods act through their organizations. The organizations of marginal people can use this distorted perception of themselves to keep their opponents off balance, to create surprises, and to maintain the initiative.

Psychology of the Organizational Process

The preceding considerations lead to an overview of the psychology of the organizational process involved. At the outset, a psychological conflict occurs within the personalities of marginal persons. They have been objects to the acting community, defined as inferior, and these definitions control the situation of poverty and enter into the image that marginal people have of themselves. Conflicting with these degrading definitions are the tendencies by marginal people to see themselves as valuable, able, and equal to anyone else.

With the initial stages of organizational effort, marginal people ward off the definitions of their inferiority and act on the basis of assumptions about their potential equality within the acting community. Now the conflict, which was located within the personalities of marginal people, becomes an objective contradiction within the object community between the organizations of marginal people and their opponents. Two consequences follow: First, motivation is released as marginal people are freed from the internal conflict that previously sapped their energies; second, it becomes more and more difficult for groups in the majority community to continue to define marginal people as inferior, in the face of increasing and highly visible evidence to the contrary.

Gradually, dissenters who see marginal people in a different and better light emerge in the majority community. Gradually, also, the organizations of marginal people create internal personality conflicts in members of the majority community—a conflict between the two warring conceptions of the nature of marginal people. When marginal people cure the majority population of this internal psychological conflict by destroying the definition of marginal people as inferior, then the marginal groups will have entered the acting community on a basis of equality.

The preceding discussion is concerned with the psychological implications of the *possibility* that marginal neighborhoods can successfully create social action organizations. We will next consider the process of the formation and functioning of such organizations.

A community development specialist, in this context an organizer, enters a marginal neighborhood as a stranger.[21] He presents himself to the neighborhood as having skills that are useful if the neighborhood wishes to organize to affect the most immediate and acutely felt grievances and secure major long-run changes.

An organizer must not only perceive how people are, but it is also essential that he be *unrealistic* in that he perceives people as they can be. Noting what is possible, the organizer projects this possibility and moves people to accept it and to seek to realize it. The organizer helps people to develop and live in an alternative reality in which their image of themselves and their abilities is enhanced. At first, therefore, the organizational process is artificial, since the alternative reality is still congealing. People are moved to accept the new world of which they catch a glimpse because it appears to be attainable in practice and intrinsically superior to the world in which they have been living. The organization through which the neighborhood acts will very likely have clear and distinct boundaries that separate those moving toward the new reality from those not making any such effort.

The organizer is not only unrealistic, but he is also *inflexible* where the necessary requirements of organizational success are concerned. The organizer does not fashion the new reality, but he does ensure that one is fashioned. He does not decide how the organization chooses to make decisions, but he does insist that it select some decision method that will be consistent with

21. For a theoretical analysis of this process, see Alfred Schutz, "The Stranger," in *Collected Papers*, II (New York: William S. Heinman, 1964), 91–105.

effective action in a long struggle and with widespread neighborhood support. The organizer will therefore help the organization to understand what he will or will not do under what conditions. He controls and maintains his own definition to the neighborhood and the limits within which he will help the neighborhood to organize.

Since the organization has to perform complex functions of planning and decision-making, in which the work must be parceled out to various people in accordance with their abilities and interests, it must have a formal or informal structure to coordinate and divide the work. Since the organization will be involved in a long struggle with powerful opponents, a struggle in which the situation will often be undefined, there will be a need for constant improvisation and a vulnerability to confusion and demoralization. For this reason, the organization should have a clear structure of authority and should develop discipline and self-responsibility among its members. The organizer ensures that such general criteria can be met, but the members of the organization decide how they want concretely to meet the requirements.

At first the organization has only a faint notion of what it is to do. It is through a process of conversation and disputation and regulated conflict with opponents that the alternative reality congeals and is related to underlying more fundamental principles. To say that an alternative reality congeals, a new world crystallizes, is to say that the organization gradually defines the marginal or undefined aspects of its situation. That is, the organization creates new relationships with opponents and others on a new basis and gradually marks out the steps it will take on this new basis.

The fact that the new situation is initially undefined may make the early stages of organization frustrating and puzzling to someone who has in mind a model of how other organizations function. An established nonconflict organization would long ago have defined the most crucial enduring aspects of its situation and usually would have defined routine reactions in such areas. The result would be that such an organization could make decisions effortlessly and concentrate on carrying them out. A newly formed organization of marginal people is in an entirely different position. Fundamental aspects of the situation are being redefined in ways that cannot be determined in advance, thus allowing only simple actions to be successfully undertaken at first. The meetings in which decisions are presumably being made are likely not to proceed in a straightforward fashion; rather, the consensus of assumptions that make collective decisions possible must be developed. Thus, much time is spent developing a consensus about what is happening and its meaning—an occupation that is the primary task of an organization of marginal people in its early stages.

A meeting during this stage progresses in unpredictable ways and at an unpredictable pace. For example, the organization may, after long discussion, make a decision and presumably settle a question. But immediately afterward it becomes clear that someone or some group misunderstood the decision, that there are various understandings of it, or that much of the membership has continued to think about the decision and now wishes to reconsider it. The question then will be taken up again; meetings may become interminable; no decisions at all may result from some meetings. The process stumbles back repeatedly while members form a common definition of the situation.

The preoccupation with reality construction can come to make meetings unpleasant and reduce action to virtually nothing. It is one of the most challenging tasks for the organizer to ensure that meetings are enjoyable enough so that the membership does not, out of frustration, desert the new organization. The organizer may do this by talking with committees or small informal central groups of members before the meeting about the problems likely to arise so that they will have some time to think them through before the meeting takes place. Gradually, a leadership nucleus develops—a nucleus that has collectively defined the situation more thoroughly than has the general membership—and this nucleus will be able to hasten the process by presenting the alternative reality to the remainder of the community. As time passes, the outcome of action in which the organization engages will support or refute the early collective definitions and lead to continual reformulation of the new reality. After a time, the organization learns to anticipate increasingly well the outcomes of its action and the process of basic reality reformulation declines in importance.

ORGANIZATIONAL EXPANSION AND DECLINE. Another common characteristic of an organization of marginal people usually comes to puzzle and frustrate those associated with it. It is that an initial period of success and expansion may be followed by a severe decline in membership and morale until it is widely feared that the new organization will disappear altogether— and well it may.

At first, people are drawn to the organization in part by curiosity, by the fact that they have not yet experienced the difficult organizational process, and by the fact that everything seems possible if there are no guidelines from past experience. But it soon is apparent that organizational work is only sometimes interesting and exciting; more often it is tedious and frustrating. Early actions also are usually undertaken without much understanding of opponents, who may quickly develop tactics to ward off the attacks. From these and similar causes the organization starts a downward course.

The downward surge accelerates by virtue of the fact that some members who thought that everything could be won quickly or not at all now believe that all is lost. It also accelerates with the departure of those who joined the organization when it looked like it would succeed and who now abandon it under the assumption that it is losing. In some ways this downward spiral benefits the new organization. The nucleus that continues its efforts despite reverses will provide more stable, long-run leadership for the organization, provided it does not remain isolated, than would some of the spectacular early careerists who entered the organization without becoming normatively affiliated with it.

But the organization continues more or less rapidly to fall apart; morale plummets. The hope that was strong at first may now virtually disappear. Those remaining members who used to see themselves as leading a mighty crusade now find themselves to be a little knot of relatively isolated people struggling against apparently insurmountable odds.

At this point other forces may come into play to restore the organization. Some people, seeing again the reality to which they are condemned if the organization disappears, say: "Here we stand, with our organization, no matter what!" Many of these people have not been central to the early effort and are not overwhelmed by that apparent failure. The nucleus remaining from the early leadership has now acquired a lengthened time perspective and has examined earlier mistakes in order to develop more successful strategies. Feeling that the battle has been won, the opponents of the organization turn their attention back to the normal conduct of their affairs.

A nucleus of greater wisdom than before extends a vision of what is possible to an increasingly restive population. The new strategies arouse hope within the organization and sidestep the means by which opponents previously defeated the organization. A resurgence begins and picks up steam. A downward slump may begin again later and the process may repeat itself at generally ascending levels of effectiveness for many years.

The foregoing account, of course, describes a common experience of a successful organization of marginal people. It is likely that if the organization lacks an experienced organizer it will not survive the first slump or will survive it as a permanent but irrelevant relic of the early effort.

The most obvious ways for an organization to defeat an opponent are through the exercise of political and economic power. However, there are also various psychological strategies more appropriate to the subject matter of this paper that we can illustrate briefly.

Suppose that the organization wishes to change some practice of the opponent. The organization first searches for moral principles or rules that the practice violates and to which the opponent might be or might become committed. The organization then helps the opponent to commit himself to those principles publicly, visibly, and sweepingly, without calling attention yet to the practice the organization wishes to change. The organization may question the extent to which the opponent really believes the principles he has enunciated and thus lead the opponent to as firm and total a commitment as possible. The opponent may even be led to bear witness to his principles as he repudiates the "smear campaign" or "rumor campaign" he asserts has been launched to harm his reputation. The organization may force the opponent not merely to announce his adherence to the principle, but to act in inexpensive ways to back up that announcement. When the opponent appears firmly enough committed to the principle in question, the organization then applies it to the practice it wants changed and threatens a public exposé of the opponent if he does not apply the principle consistently. The organization may gain only a minor tactical advantage—or it may gain a major victory.

Similarly, if an organization wishes to divest an opponent of one of his principles, the organization may first get the opponent firmly committed to principles and practice inconsistent with the one in question, and then threaten to point out the inconsistency. Even if the opponent does not abandon the principle, he will be under increased tension when attempting to act on its basis.

The organization of marginal people carries a shield of protective symbols to ward off attacks. The organization seeks publicly and privately to display a degree of virtue that opponents cannot match. Its membership will be self-responsible, honest, and virtuous in presenting itself to the majority community. The invulnerability thereby gained is heightened to the extent to which the public presentation accurately reflects the reality behind it.

The organization may continue its struggle for decades of victories and defeats but with gradually increasing power, until finally the acting community can no longer hold the marginal population outside. At that point the momentum acquired during the struggle will carry the marginal population to a desirable position within the acting community, which thereupon becomes more nearly instrumental to the creation of a good life for all the members of the object community.

EVALUATION

Finally, let us distinguish authentic community development from other kinds of effort that have received the same name. The acting community that employs a person called "community development specialist" to promote and rationalize its already formulated policies is not usually engaged in community development. That employee, who uncritically persuades a neighborhood to accept an urban renewal conservation program without seriously and critically trying to estimate whether the proposed program would actually develop the community, is not carrying out the responsibilities of his official title. Many community development positions are only disguised forms of assistance for the interests of special groups, and there are not a large number of career opportunities for those who wish to practice authentic community development. On the other hand, many persons whose efforts are not usually described as community development may, in fact, be engaged in authentic community development work.

To sum up, authentic community development programs may appear in many varieties, and the program of any one variety is likely to appear different in each of the various communities in which it appears. This fact creates a psychological difficulty in evaluation, since there is a tendency for observers to ignore the goals held by the community development specialist in question and to consider some one effort as a model. As a result, observers find it difficult to distinguish differences among programs from deficiencies of programs that differ from the model.

CHAPTER 5

The Community Development Process

DANIEL J. SCHLER

> It appears to us that a community which organizes its activity
> so that it maximizes the number of healthy, intelligent, self-
> directing citizens, capable of viewing situations from per-
> spectives other than their own, of weighing alternatives and
> making decisions, of defining new goals and inventing ways
> of achieving them, is in fact a democratic community and is
> producing members who can sustain it against all more pes-
> simistic theories of human nature and the social order. (Foote
> and Cottrell)[1]

> The day before yesterday men followed unconsciously what
> we call Nature. Yesterday men complied with nature carefully
> and candidly. Today our power of action has developed in
> such a way that we no longer rely on regulations external to
> our own deeds. It belongs to us at times to protect nature, at
> times to set it on more favorable ways. We are in a sense
> responsible for evolution. (Gaston Berger)[2]

The twentieth century may be characterized as a period of
application and experimentation with the pent-up ideas and
hopes for human and social improvement. Community development is one among many of these efforts to intentionally
improve the living conditions of people throughout the world.
Cutting a slice through the prolific literature in this field and
the many action programs that might be described, this chapter
is devoted to a theoretical and analytical discussion of the community development process as a normative methodology of
planned change.[3]

1. Nelson N. Foote and Leonard S. Cottrell, Jr., *Identity and Interpersonal Competence* (Chicago: The University of Chicago Press, 1955), 60.
2. J. R. Boudeville, *Problems of Regional Economic Planning* (Chicago:
Aldine Publishing Company, 1965), 14–15.
3. Warren Bennis, Kenneth Benne, and Robert Chin, *The Planning of
Change: Readings in the Applied Behavior Sciences.* Look for a descrip-

In order to accomplish the task of both limiting and describing community development as one type of process to induce change, a theoretical model has been constructed from the literature. Its conceptualization is at a very low level, so as to allow the inclusion of a great deal of the specific content found in most programs. From this model, a general model has been developed to delineate more clearly the procedure, content, and human interaction processes involved in the community development process. The latter sections of this chapter deal with the tendencies for change as a result of the interaction of the procedure and content of the community development process with established social systems.

Particularly since The Enlightenment, serious thought has been given to the rational direction of society. The combination of the radical ideas regarding the rights of individuals expressed in democratic theory and the development of social science as an intellectual instrument to understand and interpret human behavior and social organization, has provided the value context and method for much of modern-day intentionally created change. The ideas and theories of early scholars in these two areas of concern had to wait until the twentieth century before they were integrated and applied in massive experimental programs.

One of the first systematic statements of planned change in the United States was developed by Lester Ward in the latter part of the nineteenth century.[4] For Ward, the whole meaning of civilization lay in the triumph of artificially created social processes and structures over the natural and spontaneous development of society. He proposed the principle of "meliorism" as a means of improving social conditions through the application of scientific intelligence, and "sociocracy" as the political form of government organization for human improvement.[5] Through the distribution of wealth, power, and knowledge

tion of eight different species of change in the article, "A Typology of Change Processes," 154–56.

4. Lester F. Ward, *Dynamic Sociology*, II (New York: D. Appleton & Co., 1897); *Applied Sociology* (Boston: Ginn and Company, 1906); *The Psychic Factors of Civilization* (Boston: Ginn and Company, 1897).

5. Ward, *Psychic Factors*, 120–325.

by political systems, Ward optimistically predicted that man would be able to create intelligently a social order vastly superior to any that might result from unplanned change.

Ward's ideas and proposals were both optimistic and radical for the time in which he lived, but today they are being broadly applied and have become almost commonplace. Intentionally created change has become one of the major activities of most social systems. Governmental units, particularly, devote much time and resources to creating and supporting structures and processes that have as their immediate or long-range goal the improvement of society. Especially since the Russian revolution of 1917, the national governments in Europe and North America have given serious attention to methods of speeding up the development of various segments of society and rectifying the problems created by change or lack of change between aggregates and systems within national structures. In like manner, as new nations have emerged out of colonial status since the end of World War II, major resources have been channeled into developmental efforts. In support of the desire for rapid change, public and private foreign aid from the more developed countries has been given in unprecedented amounts to bolster the campaign for modernization around the world.

As a result of the desire for increased change and the availability of resources for such programs, the opportunity to experiment with intentionally created change has rapidly accelerated in the latter half of the twentieth century. One of the approaches applied in the developing countries has been that of the community development process. Under the guidance of European and American technical advisers, national community development programs have been designed for the explicit purpose of reaching and involving rural villagers in the nation-building process of newly emerging modern political systems.[6] While one finds national and cultural variations in the many different change programs that have been organized,

6. One United Nations definition states, "The term 'community development' has come into international usage to connote the processes by which the efforts of the people themselves are united with those of governmental authorities to improve the economic, social and cultural conditions of communities, to integrate these communities into the life of

some general characteristics of the community development process can be observed in what shall be described as the "classical approach."[7]

A CLASSICAL APPROACH

In the classical approach, the community development process has its beginning external to the villages and communities of the country. Community development technical advisers, who generally operate from American and European systems of foreign aid, provide the motivation, "know-how," and often the major resources for the establishment and organization of a nationwide program for intentionally created change. The program itself may begin as a pilot project in selected areas of the country with plans for expansion on a nationwide scale as public support builds and resources become available.

OBJECTIVE OF THE COMMUNITY DEVELOPMENT SYSTEM. The primary objective of the community development system is to make personal contact with villagers in order to assist them in learning attitudes and competencies to bring about their own development. A rational, bureaucratic system divided into spe-

---

the nation, and to enable them to contribute fully to national progress." For a more detailed statement on this position, see United Nations, Department of Economic and Social Affairs, *Community Development and National Development* (New York: United Nations, 1963), 4.

7. Materials on national programs in Africa, Asia, and Latin America have been used to construct the model describing the classical approach to community development. Some summary appraisals of these programs can be found in Ernest F. Witte, "Community Development in Selected Countries," in *Community Development Review*, 7, No. 1 (June, 1962); William Biddle and Arthur Dunham, *Currents in Community Development* (Columbia, Missouri: Department of Community Development, University of Missouri, 1964); *Report of the Inter-Regional Conference on Community Development and Its Role in Nation Building* (Seoul, Korea, 1961); *The SEATO Seminar on Community Development* (Bangkok, Thailand, July, 1963); Carl Taylor and others, *India's Roots of Democracy, A Sociological Analysis of Rural India's Experience in Planned Development Since Independence* (New York: Frederick A. Praeger, Inc., 1965).

cific functional areas such as training, operations, research, and technical support, is employed as a means of establishing and facilitating the community development process.

At the national and regional levels it is necessary to create sets of cooperative social relationships between various public and private systems to support the local process and to train, develop, and supply human and technical resources to the front-line activity. In this context, the community development process begins to modify the social values and institutions of a given country in the initial stage of launching a development program. It is argued by technicians that when the program is properly organized and administered, there will be a continuous process of institutional change throughout the country in response to meeting the needs of villagers and the development of responsive institutions to a participating national society.

Often, decentralization of services, resources, decision-making, and power occurs as the national community development program begins and becomes operationalized throughout the country. Of primary importance is the building of an effective linkage of communication and resources from the larger society to the various villages. Basic to the success of community development is the securing, integrating, and managing of resources necessary to support local development enterprises.

INSTITUTIONAL RESOURCES OF A COMMUNITY DEVELOPMENT SYSTEM. The resources required to assure systematic, orderly development of villages and communities throughout a given country may or may not be in one unit or agency and may be public or private. The main concern is that these resources are readily available to the people in the villages and are provided in keeping with the objectives and procedures of the national development program.

These resources consist basically of: (1) community workers whose primary tasks are to contact villagers, stimulate in them a desire for change, and teach them how to initiate and manage the various changes that become commonly defined within their local systems; (2) specialists in various fields of technology and service who respond to the people's requests for knowledge and assistance that may contribute to local development; (3) financial and material resources to complement and supplement local resources upon the request of the people.

The proper arrangement and management of the different types of resources employed in the development process are in themselves critical variables in the outcome of any local program. Some key principles used to guide the employment of resources to realize community development goals are:

1. train workers and develop their competence to plan and work with people rather than plan for and direct the people's actions;

2. start programs of action with problems and issues the people can identify as relevant and significant to themselves;

3. allow flexibility in programming. Emphasis is placed on fitting external resources to local designs rather than implanting national programs in local systems;

4. integrate various specialties into the service of the total community, such as agriculture, animal husbandry, public health, education, home economics, and work with women, children, and youth. The various specialists support the cooperative and collaborative efforts of local leadership in developing their own communities and community systems rather than in focusing upon developing systems that have external relationships before they become integrated into the local community system;

5. deal with change as a process of learning, rather than as a program to be imposed through top-down administration. The emphasis, thus, is on training leadership and providing experiences for learning how to work, plan, and implement programs relative to the people's own interests and needs. The community as such becomes a setting for participant experimentation and a laboratory and classroom for learning how to change and improve those things that disturb the well-being of the people in a specific locality.

THE LOCALIZED PROCESS OF CHANGE.[8]   The basic elements of the localized process consist of: (1) a worker who performs the

8. This model seeks to demonstrate that community development is a form of social change that itself must become accepted and integrated

function of encourager and enabler of change; (2) the people of a given area; (3) the environment with which they must cope; (4) the resources they may call upon; (5) the symbolic interpretations of reality they share with each other; (6) the human reciprocal relationships they build with one another; and (7) the time dimension involved in community change and continuity. The uniqueness of each element and the manner in which they are related to one another makes for diversity in the content of the process. For example, the way people interpret a problem at one time may lead to community conflict; at a later date, a change in perspective on the part of the people regarding the same problem may result in cooperation. In like manner, the focus of activity within the process at a given stage may be on agricultural improvement practices, but at a later period it may shift to changing the relationships between landowners and tenants.

In spite of the diversity that may occur in the content, it is possible to develop understanding of the general framework of action by analyzing what the worker does in initiating and encouraging human interaction for purposes of creating change. The community development process in the localized context can best be described as a normative social action system[9] that is conditioned and controlled to a large extent by the "staging" and "prompting" provided by the community development

---

into the life of a community. However, once accepted and institutionalized, community development becomes a method that people employ to bring about further conscious, deliberate, democratic processes of change based on two primary values: reason and freedom.

9. For a summary discussion of the concept of social action system, see George M. Beal, "Social Action: Instigated Social Change In Large Social Systems," in *Our Changing Rural Society,* James Copp, ed. (Ames: The Iowa State University Press, 1964), 233–64. The concept of normative social action systems is used in this chapter to stress the in-put of values and procedures that condition the manner in which social action is engaged and carried out in a community setting. To be more specific, community development change systems emphasize democratic values and procedures that are taught and practiced simultaneously with local goal achievements. In community settings where such values are already held and the general procedures are familiar to the people, the worker functions primarily to structure occasions for their articulation and operation, as well as to give positive reinforcement to those who so believe and act.

worker. Through participation, community members learn the values and procedures of this particular type of social action and gradually provide their own staging and prompting for carrying on the same process, with or without help of an external agent. A brief review of the activities of the front-line worker will point up the nature of this particular type of ordering and conditioning of human behavior for planned change.

The process begins when the worker enters the village and begins establishing relationships in a purposeful way to initiate and encourage conscious, deliberate development in the community by the people themselves. The worker initiates the process through communication with the villagers on a level they can comprehend, focused upon content that has meaning and purpose to them. For the worker to be successful in establishing the process of change, he must gain acceptance and support from the people from the very beginning and continue to build this fund of good will continuously. Being able to speak the language and having a desire to understand and identify with the people are critical factors in obtaining the necessary rapport to gain initial entry and to carry on effective relationships with the local population.

Early in his contacts, the worker legitimizes his presence in the village as someone who has come to help the villagers find ways to improve their conditions; but at the same time he seeks to avoid giving the impression of being *the* developer of the community. He meets as many villagers as possible, talking with them about their problems and concerns. Through careful listening to their comments and through discussion, he learns about the way of life in the village, the things they like and dislike, the problems confronting them, and the people in the community whom they designate as their leaders. As he gets to know the people and their concerns better, he concentrates on drawing the leaders together and aids them in focusing on the problems of the village.

The worker encourages a systematic discussion of problems and guides the villagers in thinking and reasoning about the most important problem to be solved first. He probes for answers from the people rather than giving solutions himself and calls their attention to the fact that they are more likely to be able to solve the small problems first than to take on too large a project. He also encourages them to work on something for which they have resources themselves rather than to expect help from outside the village.

The discussion and probing, thinking, and reasoning may go on for some time, but a specific goal is in mind—namely to support the villagers in developing a consensus and commitment to resolve a particular problem in their community. For this to occur requires time; in both formal and informal settings, the leaders discuss the problem with other villagers to initiate a dialogue that stretches through the entire communication network of the community.

If all goes well, the villagers reach a decision and the leadership expresses a commitment to action in behalf of the total community. At this point, a new phase in the process of change begins. The concern of the worker and village leaders becomes centered not only on what is to be done but, more important, also on how the action is to be taken.

The community development worker continues to encourage, probe, and support the villagers in thinking through the various aspects involved in accomplishing the task they desire. They may also call upon specialists to aid them in their thinking and planning. As they plan together the worker helps them outline and describe a program; they list the resources, discuss and assign responsibility, and set out a time schedule designating what will be done when, where, and by whom.

In their analysis and planning of action they may discover a need for additional resources beyond those the local community possesses. Here again the worker may aid in helping the villagers secure such resources from external systems. The planning and programming is simply stated and tied specifically to the knowledge and understanding of the villagers. In this phase of the process they are learning the basic elements of a new social technology.

The next phase of the process involves the implementation of the program. By this time, commitment and social relationships should have developed to the degree that the people will voluntarily perform the roles required in the action process. The community development worker participates in the action, taking part as one of the villagers. He also performs another function: The worker attempts to maintain enough objectivity toward the interaction and the sets of relationships that develop so that he can place himself in relationship to certain key people in the whole arrangement to encourage and support full performance of all people required to complete the action. When there is a breakdown in relationships, it will be the worker who will need to know where to begin the analysis and discussion with the people in order to restore momentum to the project.

If the worker's role is properly performed, the people will realize that they have themselves been primarily responsible for the success of the project. To build a bridge to future action, the worker and villagers evaluate and appraise the work that has been accomplished. The worker at this point becomes an "applauding audience," representing the outside world to the local villagers, and he encourages them on to new goals and higher levels of achievements.

EXPANSION OF THE PROCESS.   In general, the process starts with a small group (worker and village leadership), working on a relatively simple problem that may be solved in a short period of time, using primarily the community's own resources. Through the efforts of a front-line worker and community leadership, the process expands from its initial action system to an ever-increasing complex set of relationships, ordered around new values and procedures that prompt and guide people toward setting and achieving collective goals for human improvement. The worker's activities remain focused on creating settings and episodes for the people to learn new ideas and to build relations to augment change in a collaborative manner. Formal training sessions are often held to instruct village leaders in such topics as problem-solving methods, democratic procedures, and group discussion techniques, as well as specific content related to community problems.

As the people learn to discuss, reason, and act together to solve commonly defined problems, new identities, meanings, and relationships emerge among community members. On both a behavioral and social organizational level the community undergoes a process of disintegration and disorganization. To coordinate and reintegrate the community's efforts for change, the worker guides the local leadership in forming a permanent organization with which the people can identify and through which external systems can relate in dealing with the community. It is often possible that conflict will emerge as the community moves toward a new consensus or carries on the process of change in a setting of dissent. Community development literature is particularly lacking in discussing both the occurrence and use of conflict in the total realm of initiating and carrying out change. However, it may be assumed that, although the emphasis of the worker is on cooperation among all segments of a community, in those communities where diversity of values, interests, and power exists, competition and conflict among community members may also be expected.[10]

As a community formalizes its autonomy in self-direction through some type of organization, the worker's role generally shifts to helping the leadership develop and operate an ongoing system for change within the community setting. Particular attention is given to creating a structure in which all segments of the community's population are represented through the democratic elective process as well as to keeping the system open and sensitive to the community's needs. It can be anticipated that, following the revitalization of the community by the initial and more loosely structured action system, a tightening up of the leadership structure and of the program emphasis will occur.[11] In order to keep the formal organization from becoming rigid and set in either its leadership or action goals, the worker often continues to bring new sources of leadership and new problem areas into the stream of community concern and action.

After the initial surge for community change, the concern may shift to maintaining involvement and motivation and to developing sound programs through routine planning, train-

10. For an excellent analysis of community conflict, see James S. Coleman, *Community Conflict.*

11. For a discussion of revitalization movements and their relationship to community development, see Ward Goodenough, *Cooperation and Change,* 286–321.

ing, and evaluation procedures. The future of the process depends a great deal on an understanding and acceptance of its relevance to the people involved and their desire to support and carry on the effort. Local groups often continue to need assistance in the form of consultation, research, training, and financing to carry on programs of intentional change. Through local initiative, combined with outside assistance, the normative change process is applied repeatedly in new and varied settings in the community. However, each time it is applied, the previous actions have implications for the outcome of the new situation.

From a longitudinal perspective, the process can best be viewed as interspersed episodes in the ebb and flow of community life. The more often the process is applied and the broader the base of its application, the greater its influence is likely to be on institutions and the careers of persons.[12] The community development process is never all-inclusive change; it is, rather, selective change, limited to the specific variables chosen by the participants involved in the change process. In addition, change may occur as a consequence of the operation of the system for change, both within and external to the system's operations.

Taking into account both the goals sought for change and the effect of the process operations, there appear to be five major dimensions of community life in which change may be anticipated. The specific nature of these changes is always dependent upon a number of factors, but of major importance is the input for change that is mobilized by the change system and the manner in which the staging and prompting occur, relative to achieving goal-oriented change. This fact will become more evident as each of these dimensions is briefly discussed.

1. *Human competencies.*[13] As individuals within the community are encouraged to work together in the process of identifying and solving their own problems in a collaborative manner,

12. See Foote and Cottrell, *Identity and Interpersonal Competence,* 174–210, for a discussion of the developmental view that stresses the interrelatedness of human nature and the social order.

13. See Foote and Cottrell, *Identity and Interpersonal Competence,* for a discussion of the concept of "human competence" and its relation to change and problem solving.

a learning process occurs that may affect individual behavior in three different ways:

a. Intrapsychic.[14] Through the aid of a community development worker, individuals are encouraged to think and express their feelings toward the community in which they live and to direct those feelings into constructive actions beneficial both to the individual and to the larger context within which he lives. By becoming involved with other citizens in resolving the problems that are defined in common, each individual is challenged to think and feel more intensively about what he shares with others and what is important and significant to him as an individual. He thus becomes more emotionally involved with others in the affairs of the community in which he lives. When the process is successfully engaged, he learns to channel his emotional feeling into collective actions, which may lead to gratifying accomplishments rather than to failure, frustration, apathy, or alienation.[15]

b. Interpersonal competence.[16] With the guidance and assistance of a community development worker, individuals may learn more about how to take others into account and to negotiate for consensus and common goals, rather than seek to dominate through positions of power, authority, or status. Working with others provides a setting in which to experiment with controlling the outcome of the efforts of a group of people. Continuous participation in such groups provides the individual with recurring opportunities to experiment with improving his own group performance as well as aiding other individuals in their improvement.

c. Special skills for task performance. The structure that forms around the community development process is a microcosm. It thus offers to individual participants opportunities to perform functions that later may be applied in the larger

14. Cora Du Bois discusses the intrapsychic and interpersonal approach to change in "The Public Health Worker as an Agent of Socio-Cultural Change," in *The Planning of Change*, Bennis, Benne, and Chin, eds.

15. Melvin Seeman discusses the concept of alienation and its causes in the article "Antidote to Alienation—Learning to Belong," in *Trans-Action*, 3, No. 4 (May, June, 1966), 35–39.

16. The components of interpersonal competence are presented by Foote and Cottrell in *Identity and Interpersonal Competence*, 51–60.

context of society. Such task-oriented situations provide opportunities for learning to perform leadership and fellowship roles, technical skills in record keeping, assignment and administration of the use of resources, and the performance of various kinds of labor and occupational skills.

The amount of human competency growth that may occur as a result of the community development process is not fixed. Numerous variables come into play in terms of influencing the intrapsychic, interpersonal, and special skills development of each individual. One of the more important variables is the orientation of the agency that sponsors and encourages the community development process. Where an agency and its staff orient toward experimentation, and a great deal of resources and time are committed to teaching specific competencies, one may expect to find a greater increase of individual change in such programs as compared to those in which the agency's only emphasis is project completion.

2. *Scope of concern.* As an individual becomes involved with others in the process, a broadening of perspective and the development of collective concerns will most likely emerge.[17] The process not only aids the individual in seeing his own personal troubles and concerns in a broader perspective, but he also gains knowledge and values that enable him to link his concerns with those of other members of the community. As a result, community consciousness is often enhanced and collective action is made possible through the articulation of common concerns and the shared belief that change is both desirable and possible.

3. *Social technology.* Every society has its own particular and peculiar ways of getting things done. One of the implicit aspects of the community development process is that it teaches people a social technology relevant to doing those things they would like to have done. The basic elements of this social technology consist of:

a. rational goal setting in order that the actions of various individuals can be directed toward a specific target;

17. Leon H. Warshay, "Breadth of Perspective," in *Human Behavior and Social Processes,* Arnold Rose, ed. (Boston: Houghton Mifflin Company, 1962).

b. planning how to use resources in such a way as to achieve the stated goal or objective, which involves basically a process of imagining how a certain task will be done before the process is engaged;

c. rational division of labor in order that specific roles may be assigned relative to the functions that need to be performed;

d. administration and coordination of the functional units.

The various operations of the local process, even in their elementary form, encompass all preceding elements. Participants engaged in the process learn to apply this social technology with greater skill and efficiency the more they practice it. Its adoption as a major means of accomplishing action provides a given group of people with a greater amount of control over their own destiny and more efficient use of resources toward goal achievement.

4. Physical technology. Technical change is often the major goal of people involved in the community development process, but, as we have seen so far, it is certainly not the only change possible. Physical and technical changes are basic to the community development process and are generally the base around which human relationships form and action systems are created. These changes encompass the improved use of all types of resources toward the goal of human betterment. It is generally assumed that the community development process encourages and speeds up technical change, but this may not always be the case.

5. Social organization. The effects of another change, that of social organization, may be seen on two levels:

a. The reorganization of existing social systems. As a result of the operation of the community development process, new values and patterns of relationships may be introduced into the community setting that alter the old ways of doing things. For example, the family may still remain as a social unit, but its socioeconomic operations may be greatly modified as a consequence of the introduction of the ideas of equal rights for women.

It is generally assumed by social scientists that the parts of a society are interrelated and that change in one part will result in some form of alteration or adjustment in other related units.

Thus, a change in the family system may alter the values and patterns of behavior in the economic and educational institutions of the community. In like manner, one may also expect to find new patterns of relationships emerging between the various subsystems of the community as a consequence of the introduction of change in any of its components. The introduction of cash-crop farming may lead to the development of individual or family enterprise systems and the lessening of voluntary, cooperative, communal labor activities. In some cases, barter and personal relationships may be replaced by money and commercialism and by impersonal organization or reciprocal relationships.

It is impossible to assume that such reorganization and adjustments always take place in an environment of harmony or leave the community in a state of total integration. The rate of both induced change and spontaneous change in modern societies is sufficiently rapid to assume that disharmony and conflict are constant factors that must be taken into account in many community settings. The unusual community is likely to be the one where change has been dealt with in such a manner as to bring about a constant process of consensus and reintegration. This is a major goal of community development that is not easy to achieve.

b. The establishment of new institutional forms. New forms of social organization generally serve as a context within which newly defined needs are met and the scope of human activities are expanded.[18] Of particular importance in developing countries has been the creation of local governmental institutions as well as various kinds of educational and social service agencies. The extension of the formal bureaucratic society into relatively isolated communities has created whole new forms of social organization that people must learn to identify and associate with, in addition to the traditional societal forms. The complexity involved in this reorganization and reorientation

18. Warren Peterson and George Zollschan employ the concept of "need" in relation to urban change processes and describe the "institutionalization of need" as a process of social organization and reorganization in "Social Processes in the Metropolitan Community," *Human Behavior and Social Processes*, Arnold Rose, ed., 649–66.

is often not appreciated by the outsider, who may be a party to introducing rapid change into formerly relatively stable and slow-changing community systems.[19] In the more highly developed societies, intentional change has become more commonplace and tends to blend with the existing conditions of communities that are in a constant process of rapid transition.[20] In such settings, institutional forms, such as voluntary or legally established planning and coordinating bodies, are often created for the purpose of redirecting change and for engaging in building systems through which concerted, selective change can be systematically and effectively dealt with.

The institutionalization of the community development process in a local area generally involves the creation of a new organizational structure. The main system that is developed may serve any or all such functions as initiating change, planning and coordinating the efforts of a number of subsystems in programs of change, and/or operating new services designed to improve the living conditions of the people of the community. In addition, one may expect to find "satellite" and independent organizations that develop as a result of "spin-off" from the operations of the community development process.

Although the general approach of community development is to create new organizations only when required to meet human needs and to develop them in cooperation with existing institutions and agencies, it is presumptuous to assume this will always occur without arousing rivalries and possible conflict among the vested interests that may be involved. In such cases, the community development process may itself be the source of community conflict and establish the basis for a contest between different segments and interests in the community. The resolution of these differences, it is assumed by community development proponents, can be rationally negotiated in free and open discussion. However, this is a value and methodolog-

19. Margaret Mead, *Cultural Patterns and Technical Change* (Paris: UNESCO, 1953).

20. See Maurice Stein, *The Eclipse of Community* (Princeton: Princeton University Press, 1960), and Roland Warren, *The Community in America* for discussions of the rapid transition and the "great change" in American communities.

ical bias of community development that may not be achievable under all conditions.[21]

While each of these dimensions of change has been looked at separately for analytical purposes, in the real world of events changes often occur simultaneously and interact with other processes to produce additional changes in the whole configuration of a given localized human environment. As such, the community development process, engaging as it does episodically in the ebb and flow of community life, becomes one among many forces affecting the outcome and destiny of any community. The more comprehensively the process is applied and the greater the intensity of its engagement, the more likely it is to have a strong influence upon the various dimensions of community life. An understanding of how this may be achieved and the effect it produces requires a closer examination of the procedure, content, and social interactional dimensions of the community development process in its broadest context.

A General Model of the Community Development Process

As has been indicated in the discussion of the classical approach, the community development process is a specific type of social process created for the purpose of promoting locally planned change. It implies a joint effort between local leadership and external personnel and resources to attack and resolve problems so comprehensive that they are usually beyond the scope of any existing single agency. The process in the local setting may be intentionally directed toward any segment or problem in the community and as such engages episodically in selective change in the life of the community. While permanent organizational structures are sought for continuity of purpose and action, *ad hoc* systems also emerge from time to time to study, plan, and implement programs of change.

The community development process provides for the involvement and integration of a community worker and lay

21. Warren Bennis, "Theory and Method in Applying Behavioral Science to Planned Organizational Change," *The Journal of Applied Behavioral Science*, 1, No. 4 (October, November, December, 1965), 337–60.

leaders into a collaboratively planned change enterprise. It permits the use of expert advice and external resources where needed, while strongly retaining the responsibilities of local decision-making. The problems of simultaneously maintaining a balance in local decision-making and providing resources for development in many local units may create tensions and conflict among local, regional, and national systems. To lessen these conditions the front-line workers often play a strong role in orienting village leaders to the agency's program and seek to guide villagers in considering development goals in keeping with national priorities. In like manner, workers may seek to channel the needs of villagers upward through the structure so as to affect the decision-making of those who will allocate resources for development at higher levels of government. As social organization builds from the grass roots upwards and the bureaucracy decentralizes downward, integration of local communities and the national structure would be most beneficial.

To clarify what is involved in the total operation of community development, a general model has been developed to illustrate three different dimensions of the structure and relationships within it: the *procedural dimension*, which points to the importance of continuity and the sequence of events; the *content dimension*, which allows for the assessment, measurement, and evaluation of input for change; and the *human interaction dimension*, which stresses that planned change is a product of effective human interaction processes on all levels at all times.

The nature of the relationship of communities to the larger society, as discussed in Chapter 2 of this book, requires that both lay citizens and professional community development personnel view community change in terms of its internal and external relationships. For this reason, the model suggested here, dealing with creating intentional community change, includes at all stages the resource system for change, which in most cases of comprehensive change will be at least partly external from the local system. A brief discussion following the model will point up the interrelationships of the various dimensions and the systematic relationships therein.

General Model for Procedural Dimension of the Community Development Process

Stage I. Resource Organization

- Policy formulation
- Creation of bureaucratic system
- Setting out guideline for operation
- Recruitment of staff
- Training of workers
- Creation of a research and evaluative system

Stage II. Engagement of Resource System with a Community Unit

- Decentralization of operations
- Local reconnaissance surveys
- Creation of local arrangements for contact, program development, and implementation

Stage III. Activating a Local Goal-Oriented System

- Creating a setting and situation for democratic discussions
- Systematic discussions of community-felt needs
- Fact-finding
- Assessment of problems
- Setting goal proprieties
- Planning for action
- Implementation and resource application
- Evaluation

Stage IV. Operation of the Local System

- Organization of ongoing system
- Provision for staff and lay citizens' training in human relations and program content areas
- Establishment of an evaluative and operative research system
- Standardization of relationships with external and internal community systems for securing resources
- Development of a standard operating procedure including management and control over the operations of the system
- Establishment of a development research system to discover new problems and approaches to change
- Provision for intake of new resources from external and internal community sources through program development and management

General Model for Content (Input) Dimension of the Community Development Process

Stage I. Resource Organization

- Utilization of CD and Administration personnel to assist in organization

- Utilization of CD and technical specialist in proposed program areas for training

Stage II. Engagement of Resource System with a Community Unit

- Use of administrative personnel in decentralizing the operation
- Use of local level workers to establish contact with communities
- Utilization of CD workers' skills on community analysis and organization

Stage III. Activating a Local Goal-Oriented System

- Utilization of communication and democratic group process skills by CD workers
- Utilization of technical specialists to aid in problem clarification and possible solutions
- Securing and employing internal and external resources
- Programming for task assignment and resources application
- Use of CD workers' human relations skills to encourage the people to act
- Review of problem-solving process to create understanding of accomplishments and possible mistakes

Stage IV. Operation of the Local System

- Utilization of organizational and system management skills
- Continuous use of research skill
- Continuous use of program planning skills
- Utilization of CD workers' skills to involve lay citizens in continuous problem-solving process
- Utilization of specialists and technicians in program areas
- Continuous use of evaluative skills and techniques

General Model for Human Interaction Dimension of the Community Development Process

Stage I. Resource Organization

- Creation of awareness and understanding of CD
- Negotiation for support
- Building a system of continuous support
- Establishing relationships for recruitment of staff
- Clarifying the purpose and procedure of operation

Stage II. Engagement of Resource System with a Community Unit

- Working out vertical relations within the bureaucratic structure
- Getting accepted in communities
- Creating an awareness and need for CD
- Talking to people to find out the problems and issues of the community and whom they look to for leadership
- Building relationships for local legitimation and sponsorship

- Getting broad representation on the community participation system

Stage III.   Activating a Local Goal-Oriented System

- Allowing for broad citizen participation and involvement
- Achieving effective communication and discussion-decision processes
- Determining means for getting information from inside and outside the community
- Broadening the perspectives and self-interests
- Creating an understanding of problems and possibilities for solution
- Learning to take others into account
- Getting agreement and commitment to a specific goal for action
- Maintaining interests to work out details
- Developing realistic group aspirations for accomplishment
- Building cooperative and collaborative relationships
- Assessing personal and group successes and failures

Stage IV.   Operation of the Local System

- Determining the appropriate organizational mechanism for continuous operations
- Clarifying the central purpose and function of the change system within the community structure
- Working out the system's organizational arrangement within the community and externally
- Working out an equitable representation of the various segments of the community
- Establishing *ad hoc* systems to broaden the base of participation
- Assuring lay citizens' involvement and group achievement to create motivation for change
- Constructive use of conflict to redirect purpose, content, or operation of the change system

Stage I. Resource Organization. The *procedure* involves the establishment and operation of a system of resources for change. It includes setting up the organizational structure, defining the purpose and guidelines of operation, delineating the areas of action, developing time schedules, securing the appropriate staff and finances, and "building-in" a system of evaluation.

The *content* requires a consideration of the availability of resources for change and the utilization of a bureaucratic system oriented toward program development from the bottom up. Provision must also be made for the effective and efficient use of trained specialists who can plan action programs with lay citizens. Likewise, technical consultants and personnel are needed to plan and operate training programs for all levels of staff, with primary emphasis on local workers in the beginning phases.

The *human interaction* dimension takes into account the necessity of creating an understanding of the need for community development and the negotiations required of a multiplicity of interests to gain broad support for the community development operation. Some structural arrangement is often necessary to achieve and maintain the involvement of significant agencies and leaders to assure the necessary legitimation. On another level, proper communication needs to exist to allow for the recruitment, selection, training, and assignment of staff to positions in the bureaucratic structure.

Stage II. Engagement of the Resource System with a Community Unit. The *procedure* calls for the recognition of the complexity of community life and the lack of any one structure that represents the interests of all aggregates. A method must be devised for finding a body of individuals through which the resources can be effectively related to major segments of the community.

The *content* dimension stresses the training of community level workers in understanding community structure and in developing skills in research methods for determining the particular nature of a community's organization and leadership patterns.

The *human interaction* dimension indicates that local differences in community structure and leadership should help shape the manner in which the resource system is related to the community unit. Standardization of structure may be sought, but flexibility must likewise be maintained to give room for local variations in leadership and human interaction patterns.

Stage III. Activating a Local Goal-Oriented System. The *procedure* points up the common elements in social action systems.[22] Models of social action are important in gaining an appreciation of the need to carry through stages of action for success.

22. George M. Beal, "Social Action: Instigated Social Change in Large Social Systems," in *Our Changing Rural Society*, James H. Copp, ed. (Ames: The Iowa State University Press, 1966), 233–64.

The *content* dimension emphasizes the role of the community worker and other technical aids in guiding interested citizens through the initial problem-solving process into action. This includes the problems of definition and clarification, study, fact-finding, goal selection, training, planning, programming, and implementation.

The *human interaction* dimension stresses the importance of good communication and discussion-decision processes inside and outside the system throughout the entire procedure. Particular attention should be given to the process of reaching an agreement on the action objectives and the method of achievement.

Stage IV. Operation of the Local System in Cooperation and Collaboration with Internal and External Systems. The *procedure* emphasizes the need for continuity in intentionally-created community change programs. While *ad hoc* systems are a vital part of the ongoing nature of any social system, the reality of community problems requires more permanence than the episodic change programs of the past. To build this type of permanence into community structures requires the continuous maintenance of a series of operations.[23]

The *content* dimension calls for a continuous critical examination of the goal of the system in terms of the need for community change. It also suggests the need for built-in evaluation, which provides a continuous feedback regarding the effectiveness of the system in terms of the creation and operation of programs, or the coordination and integration of functions.

The *human interaction* dimension points up the need for creating stability in the organization and in its relationship to the community. It is important to build in new leadership, fresh approaches to old problems, and opportunities for learning experiences for all who become involved.

With the increased problems facing community leaders brought on by the speed of change itself, some permanent mechanism for creating and directing intentional change seemed

23. For a discussion of the various operations necessary for continuity and effectiveness of a program of change, see Irwin Sanders, "Community Development Programs in Sociological Perspective," in *Our Changing Rural Society*, James H. Copp, ed., 307–40.

needed. The model presented here attempts to encompass the vertical and local relationships involved in such change systems, and it also demonstrates the three primary dimensions that constitute their structure. Finally, attention needs to be given to the kind of by-products or residues that may be expected to occur in social systems as a result of initiating and carrying out the community development process.

Basic Change Tendencies

In the classical community development approach there is a definable and generally accepted set of traditions that contains points to be emphasized in the practice of community development. In some community development literature these traditions are dealt with as principles. We shall treat them as tendencies for change that result in residues in social systems where community development programs are carried out.

Five tendencies have been delineated for analysis and discussion:

1. *Toward prospective goal setting.* Social scientists have long been engaged in the process of making studies of economic and social trends and projecting these trends into the future. Various programs of change have been built around forecasts to smooth out the cyclical fluctuations that occur.

Community development has been involved in a different kind of developmental programming. Although it builds upon forecasting and upon observing past trends and fluctuations, a critical difference lies in the goal-setting mechanism that occurs in community development. Prospective goal setting is different from projection, in that it embodies the development of policy and the creation of public support for planning and carrying out the necessary action to achieve the goal that has been established. Such goal setting and achievement are not to deny the validity of economic variables that set limits on what is possible at any given time. However, the major factor involved in this process is the negotiation of social objectives within the realm of technical and economic possibilities.

New forces are brought to bear upon development when prospective goal setting is introduced into the thinking and actions of people. These goals activate resources that may otherwise not have been employed, such as the unused labor resources where underemployment exists. Also, with prospective goal setting, certain activities can be directed toward a given goal with more efficiency and accuracy.

The implication is that conditioning of people to think in terms of rational goal setting within the context of the community unit and experimenting and learning that change is possible are implicit to the process. Success in goal achievement strongly supports the development of a positive attitude toward change and the reduction of fatalistic beliefs.

2. *Toward self-help and self-development.* Community development is based upon the philosophy of self-help and participation by as many members of the community as possible. The tendency to focus on self-initiative and self-responsibility may give rise to creativity directed toward improvement. It becomes the antithesis of a dependent society in which the individual actors wait for some external stimulus to trigger the process of change to which they then respond.

The conditioning of individuals to channel their actions into collective forms is further influenced by the community development process that stresses mutual aid and the building of collaborative relationships. The individual's own desire for action and self-help is channeled into joint enterprises with others. Through this guided experiment the individual is aided in working and living cooperatively with others in realizing common goals. Through the exercise of mutual aid in cooperative endeavors the individual may likewise come to recognize and appreciate the value of reciprocal relationships as a means of improving his own welfare.

3. *Toward the democratization of human relationships.* The tendency to emphasize democratic philosophy and procedures in the community development process may be transferred into other settings of the community. Open election of people to positions of leadership, taking other people into account in decision-making, and jointly deciding on who will play designated leadership roles are exercises in democratic practice that in general may lead toward the democratization of human relations.

Efficiency in organizations can be achieved through rational bureaucracies. But bureaucracies require hierarchies of authority and systems of control over their various subunits. Thus, there are constant tendencies for greater control and regimentation over the lives of individuals as scientific and bureaucratic procedures are more extensively applied in any given society.

The community development process is not a panacea for a world threatened by new types of authoritarianism, nor is it a bulwark for individual freedom. However, there is a definite input of democratic values, principles, and procedures that, when applied in various settings of society, can be expected to loosen rigid social structures. When the individuals who control these structures refuse to change in keeping with the needs and desires of the majority of the people, the existence of democratic ideas and values may serve to change these structures by replacing those who are in control.

4. Toward rationality in decision-making. Central to the process of technical and social change are the choices and decisions that individuals make in the process of satisfying their perceived wants and needs. The criteria used for the allocation of resources to meet human needs are often subject to traditional values held in common by people in a given society. Community development implicitly seeks to provide new criteria by which to make these decisions. Whenever possible, emphasis is placed on the use of valid knowledge as a substitute for conventional wisdom or pressure tactics. The result of this tendency can be expected to increase the application of professional and scientific knowledge in decision-making processes.

5. Toward concerted decision-making and action systems. In order for rational decision-making to be realized in the community setting, certain structural arrangements are necessary. First, there must be an explicit system, encompassing the total community, that is able to develop understanding and judgments regarding the welfare of all. Second, once a decision is made, the various subsystems within the community should abide by the concerted decision. The community development process attempts both to aid in the creation of the structure within which the decision is made and to develop the public support and understanding through which a voluntary response to the collective decision-making process may be made. In some cases, external procedures may need to be developed in order to coordinate and integrate the actions of various systems toward the realizing of over-all community goals.

It is evident from community development case studies that these tendencies appear to be present to some extent in any program that stresses the initiation, reinforcement, and carrying through of the community development process in a local setting. Thus, inherent in the process itself and in the content that usually accompanies it are tendencies to produce certain kinds of behavioral and organizational patterns.

Those who study the effects of community development programs over long periods of time would be well advised to include evaluative instruments to determine to what degree prospective goal setting, self-help, joint enterprise endeavors, democratic human relationships, and rational-concerted decision-making and action have become institutionalized into the over-all structure of a community system. Those who propose intentionally created change may likewise want to consider the tendencies for behavioral and social change that the community development process implies, for no method of change can be applied without leaving its effects upon those who are changed. The method itself becomes an end product in the whole configuration of change. Upon closer observation it may be discovered that the residual results are more important for human survival in the long run than the immediate goals. Those who diligently practice the community development process may be creating the conditions for community development described by the two quotations at the beginning of this chapter.

Part Three of this volume centers on the role of the two major participants in the process—the citizen and the community developer. To say that the people of a community should actively participate in the process is not sufficient. Beyond the important observation made by Haggstrom that certain marginal groups seldom enter into the process, we need to recognize that most groups participate only in restricted ways and only for limited periods of time. Sutton notes that, because the process frequently lasts so long and moves so slowly, many citizens, even those interested in the activity, have difficulty in maintaining interest and following the course of events.

The community development process is carried out through one of three major organizational models: (1) the inclusive organization, which provides for direct participation but is restricted to relatively small villages or limited urban neighborhoods; (2) the representative organization, which, of necessity, participates indirectly and, therefore, suffers from specific problems built into the concept of representation; and (3) the nonrepresentative organization, which is the most commonly employed model. Frequently, representative organizations are not representative at all. The concept of representation should be limited to the *authorized* functioning for others in order that it become a more meaningful term in the literature. Other major issues affecting the representative organization are the relationships between the subgroups and the larger organization and the lack of involvement of marginal groups.

When discussing citizen participation in community development at least three important needs and areas for additional emphasis come to the fore. The first of these needs is the indigenous recognition of community development organizations as both legitimate and representative of the community; second is the need to involve marginal groups more fully in such organizations; third is the need to develop new models of participation that take the collective identity concept of community and the temporal and continuity aspects of process into account.

Along with the citizen, the community developer is the other major participant in the process. In Chapter 7, Morris suggests that the most troublesome question is whether the community developer does have an identifiable set of skills that distinguishes him from other professionals and differentiates him from the citizen. If so, we need to identify and specify these skills more clearly and to describe the various types of community development roles more adequately.

The value foundations for development tasks are rather easy to identify but somewhat difficult to translate into specific skills and to apply in actual situations. While the major elements of community development, mentioned several times throughout the book, apply here, the reality of employment by an organization external to the community where the process will occur raises serious questions.

Terms like *enabler, organizer,* and others are frequently used to describe the underlying philosophical thrust of the community developer's role. Morris establishes four roles, based on the central practical tasks that are performed by the developer. The four he identifies are: (1) the field agent; (2) the adviser or consultant; (3) the advocate; and (4) the planner. Applicable to all four roles is the task of integrating the expressed wants of the citizens with the externally derived knowledge and insights of the community developer.

Morris expects a wholly new and free-standing professional or technical skill to develop that will define the developer and his roles more clearly than is true now. In terms of the present reality of development practice, most community developers either combine a technical skill with the development function or serve as a development specialist on a team or project that has rather explicit aims and objectives. In the latter half of his chapter, Morris discusses the methods of the community developer and some of the major employers of the development worker. In the final section he reviews some of the conflicts and contradictions that confront the developer, including the balance between social change and cultural preservation, time sense and tempo, and the relationship between local development needs and outside plans and resources.

It is important to add that a number of relatively new resources are helping to bring community development to professional status. The University of Missouri–Columbia, and Southern Illinois University at Carbondale both offer graduate education leading to masters' degrees in community development. A number of other institutions have either undergraduate or graduate courses in the area, and some offer annual seminars and workshops for specific audiences. Support for professional education in community development, usually in the form of financial aids and awards to students, is now being provided by a number of departments and agencies of government. A new individual membership association for the professional advancement of community development was formed early in 1969, and several older national and international organizations offer a forum to the community developer. Much more needs to be done to ensure professional definition and status for this special area, but most people active in community development would agree with Morris' prediction that a wholly new and free-standing profession is emerging. Others would argue that it is already here.

CHAPTER 6

The Role of the Citizen
in the Community Development Process

LEE J. CARY

Basic to the community development process is participation by the people of the community in the process. The emphasis is on common or shared interests and concerns—public issues —which grow out of individual interests and concerns. Ross speaks of this participation as issuing from a widely shared discontent with existing conditions, focused and channeled into organization, planning, and action.[1] Participation results from sufficient consensus concerning the desirability and the direction of change. The consensus must be strong enough to initiate a program of action that meets with the approval of a majority of those combined in the action.

The initial reason for joining together is the realization that most action taken by or on behalf of groups is undertaken through organization. Therefore, we look to organization as the vehicle through which desired change can be accomplished. We also realize, perhaps less clearly, that the community development process, when effectively employed, helps to strengthen the horizontal pattern of the community—the relationship between local units or subgroups in the community.[2] We have, therefore, two major objectives in the community development process. One is the task accomplishment of the organization— the concrete results. As Festinger points out, membership is not belonging but attaining something by belonging.[3] The oth-

1. Murray G. Ross, *Community Organization: Theory, Principles and Practice*, 158–68.

2. Roland L. Warren, *The Community in America*. See especially Chap. 9, "The Community's Horizontal Pattern: The Relation of Local Units to Each Other," 267–302, and Chap. 10, "Community Action and Community Development," 303–39.

3. Leon Festinger, "Group Attraction and Membership," in *Group Dynamics*, Dorwin Cartwright and Alvin Zander, eds. (Evanston, Ill.: Row, Peterson, 1953), 93.

er objective is the process itself and what accrues to the community through its participation in this process. The second of these two objectives, which emphasizes the community's participation in the process, will be the focus of this chapter.

Five important dimensions of participation will be presented, followed by a discussion of social participation, community leadership, and indigenous movements. A major portion of the chapter will consider three models of participation: (1) the inclusive organization, with direct participation; (2) the representative organization, with indirect participation; and (3) the nonrepresentative organization, with open participation. The final portion of the chapter will examine four components of a participative organization.

Certain value assumptions underlie the emphasis on extensive involvement and cooperative effort. The emphasis, however, does not deny the importance of individual effort nor does it preclude other approaches to the solution of community problems and the bringing about of community change. The three major value assumptions presented here are: (1) people of the community should actively participate in community change; (2) participation should be as inclusive as possible; and (3) participation should be through democratic organizations. Three necessary conditions for participation must be present if these value assumptions are to be realized: (1) freedom to participate—autonomy; (2) ability to participate; and (3) willingness to participate.

Obviously, not all people will choose to participate in community action. Many may not even be aware of the opportunity to join with others in cooperative effort. It is also clear that much change will occur whether or not the people of a community act cooperatively. This fact means that specific issues and concerns become focal points for groups, which then decide to act with respect to one or more of the specific issues to the exclusion of other issues and concerns. In the process of selecting an issue, some people will choose not to participate because of lack of interest or actual disagreement with the particular action planned or under way. Others will not participate because of an unwillingness to become involved with those who are active. Still others will involve themselves initially but later withdraw because of disagreement with the program objectives, with the way the program is being carried out, or with others who are participating.

Beginning with less than full participation on the part of the community, a number of factors (including but not limited to those cited) will tend initially to limit and later to decrease actual participation in a particular program. Equally true is the possibility that the organization will attract other members if it achieves specific objectives and gains a certain degree of strength, stability, and prestige in the community. This movement of individuals in and out of community development organizations raises the questions of organizational maintenance and the importance of organizational renewal.

The Dimensions of Participation

In discussing the community's involvement in the community development process one must consider a number of aspects of participation. Five to be discussed here are: (1) prerequisites to participation; (2) types of participation; (3) types of participants; (4) relationship of participants to locality; and (5) stages of organization as they relate to participation. An understanding of these aspects will provide some insight into the nature and extent of citizen involvement, relationship to the local community, and the relationship of participation to organizational development.

While an exhaustive discussion of prerequisites to effective participation is beyond the scope of this chapter, a most logical point of departure is to consider some of the preconditions to effective participation. Ross offers some suggestions with respect to this aspect of participation. First, and most fundamental, is a breadth of knowledge and a broad background that allow one to identify priorities and see issues in context. There is no substitute for informed citizens. Second is the ability to learn rather quickly about problems and learn enough to reach a decision. This precondition includes the ability to utilize experts effectively, to undertake self studies, and to grasp the major issues involved and the implication of various courses of action. Third is the ability to act and to act effectively. Of these three, however, the first is the most basic to effective participation.[4]

The literature of social participation will be discussed briefly in the next part of this chapter. It is sufficient here to point out that most research on social participation is limited, in that participation or membership is a quantitative and not a qualitative measure. Clearly, there is much more to participation than simply belonging, but studies on the extent of participation are meager. Chapin, over twenty-five years ago, listed five aspects of participation on his social participation scale. His measurement of participation started with membership and included, from low to high, attendance at meetings, financial contribution, membership on committees, and positions of leadership.[5]

While these aspects do not exhaust the important dimensions of participation, they do represent at least one effort to look beyond membership alone as the measure of social participation. Two other important aspects of participation include what members do *between* meetings and what part they play *during* meetings. The between-meetings participation may include a variety of tasks from typing minutes to planning strategy. Participation during meetings indicates the individual's role in the decision-making process of the organization. From experience, we know that a person without a formal leadership role frequently exerts considerable influence on the organization's decisions. Stated another way, the positional leaders are not necessarily *the* leaders of the organization. An important aspect of participation, therefore, is some involvement beyond the simple act of belonging.

While the type of participation is important, the type of participant is equally so. Sutton and Kolaja identify the actor, the recipient, and the public as three categories that identify the major constituents in the action. Whether or not these persons and groups are mainly from within or from outside the

4. Murray G. Ross, "Community Participation," *International Review of Community Development*, 5 (1960), 107–19.

5. E. Stuart Chapin, "Social Participation and Social Intelligence," *American Sociological Review*, 4 (1939), 157–66.

community—in other words, the degree of relatedness to a particular locality—is an equally important dimension.[6] The actors are those who take an active part in the action. Recipients are those whom the action has objectively affected or will affect. They may or may not be those for whom the actors intend the action. The third group, the public, are those not directly involved in the action, but who must be (or should be) taken into account by the actors.

Sanders, approaching classification of participants from the viewpoint of the person charged with the guidance and operation of the community development process, identifies four types of functionaries: local leaders; resident professionals; professional organizers from the outside; and multipurpose community development workers.[7] The first type leaves the process in the hands of local leaders, who will probably vary widely in qualifications, understanding of community development, and the time and energy devoted to the process. The resident professional usually develops and promotes a segmental community development interest such as education, social welfare, or agriculture. The outside professional organizer functions temporarily to accomplish a specific program. The multipurpose community development worker is a generalist as far as subject-matter fields go. He is a specialist in the community development process. The various roles of the community development worker or agent will be discussed in detail in Chapter 7.

The relationship of participants to locality is a relatively simple matter to determine, but it is important in understanding a community's participation in the community development process. Depending on the nature of the community development organization and the community in which it is located, one may find a large number of the participants coming from outside the community. Urban neighborhood organizations in low-income areas frequently involve a number of "outsiders" actively. Rural community development programs may

6. Willis A. Sutton, Jr., and Jiri Kolaja, "Elements of Community Action," *Social Forces*, 38 (May, 1960), 325–31.

7. Irwin T. Sanders, "Theories of Community Development," *Rural Sociology*, 23 (March, 1958), 1–12.

receive some of their support and leadership from nearby urban centers. Not all participants, therefore, may come from the local community; this is not necessarily undesirable. On the other hand, if too high a percentage of the active participants, particularly those in leadership positions, come from outside the community, then local leadership needs to be recruited and trained.

A final dimension of participation to be considered here is the stages of organizational development and the relationship between these stages and participation. Organizations created for one specific project or continuing over time tend to develop through at least three stages. There are variations in the nature and extent of participation with each stage. While various writers have identified these stages in a number of ways, I shall refer to them here simply as the initial stage of organization, the task accomplishment stage, and the stage of continuity or discontinuity.

The initial stage of organization probably involves fewer participants than the other stages. These participants discuss ideas and issues and make tentative plans for the organization. The community leaders or those most concerned about the particular matter under consideration are apt to participate at this point. The need here is for people who "know the community" well enough to identify others who ought to be involved. Persons with ideas and with the ability to implement ideas contribute heavily during this initial stage.

The task accomplishment stage usually calls for an expansion in participation. Community participation is at its highest point during this period. More people are needed in the program of action than in either the initial stage or in the stage of continuity or discontinuity. Frequently, additional participants, in such roles as interviewer, solicitor, or manual worker, are necessary to implement the program of action. In other instances, additional participation may be sought to help support the outcome of the action. In too many cases increased participation is considered a goal in itself. A broad base of participation is thought of as desirable, without considering why additional participants are being sought or how they will be involved, once they are brought into the organization.

The third stage of organization is the stage of continuity or discontinuity. If activity is to be discontinued after the completion of a single project, then participation will taper off as the organization closes down and transfers any continuing aspect of the project to some ongoing group. In most instances, however, after the organization has achieved its objective it does not dissolve but continues with new tasks to be accomplished, and participation over time assumes new and different dimensions. People lose interest and drop out. Leaders resign. New people become involved without a knowledge of the history of the organization and its earlier efforts. The nature and extent of individual participation changes over time and the membership changes over time as well.

To summarize, the people of a community should be active participants in community change; participation should be as inclusive as possible; and community change should occur through democratic organization. We have looked briefly at the dimensions of participation in terms of the nature and extent of participant activity, types of participants, the relationships between participants and the community, and between participants and the stages of organization development.

SOCIAL PARTICIPATION, COMMUNITY LEADERSHIP, AND INDIGENOUS MOVEMENTS.   As mentioned earlier, the literature on social participation, although extensive, tends to be limited in its definition of participation; it measures participation in organizations rather than participation in community. Most studies find that participation is directly related to socioeconomic position. The higher the socioeconomic status, the greater the amount of participation.[8] Participation is usually measured in terms of membership or simply "belonging," as determined by the respondent. At best, this is a limited gauge, which indicates that a

---

8. Morris Axelrod, "Urban Structure and Social Participation," *American Sociological Review*, 21 (February, 1956), 13–18; Wendell Bell and Maryanne T. Force, "Social Structure and Participation in Different Types of Formal Associations," *Social Forces*, 34 (May, 1956), 345–50; John M. Foskett, "Social Structure and Social Participation," *American Sociological Review*, 20 (August, 1955), 431–38; Basil G. Zimmer and Amos H. Hawley, "The Significance of Membership in Associations," *The American Journal of Sociology*, 65 (September, 1959), 196–201.

person considers himself a part of or at least identified with a group. It does not tell us anything about the nature or extent of his involvement.

There are at least two important implications for us in studies of social participation. First, because of differential participation patterns, decisions arrived at through these organizations reflect the interests and biases of the members, who do not fully represent the population. The base of participation is not only limited, but it is skewed in the direction of the higher socioeconomic groups. Those from the upper socioeconomic segment of the community are over-represented. Second, there is a tendency to isolate subgroups of the population, particularly the low-income segment, from effective participation in the larger community.

This unequal involvement brings us back to the second of our three value assumptions—that participation should be as inclusive as possible. Programs and projects not shared in by all segments of the community may not only jeopardize the particular action but may also bring about a reaction from the nonparticipants that goes far beyond the immediate situation. Unequal, limited participation by the community will certainly hamper the efforts to strengthen the horizontal pattern of the community and the "community integration" aspect of the process as described by Ross.

Studies of community leadership, beginning with Floyd Hunter's *Community Power Structure*, published in 1953, further support the contention that, frequently, community decisions are made and action taken by a rather small group of citizens. Studies of the reputational type typically ask a selected group of informants to name the leaders or influential members of the community. From such information the study identifies a community leadership group. Such a group tends to be a part of all important community decisions and may actually dominate the community.

More recent studies have identified not one but a number of leadership groups in the community. A community leadership study conducted in Syracuse, New York, sought to identify the groups and individuals participating in one or more of thirty-nine decisions selected as representing a broad cross-section of community action. Approximately nineteen groups were involved in the thirty-nine decisions, but *less than three-tenths of one per cent* of the adult citizens of the area participated in a direct way in the making of these thirty-nine community decisions.[9]

While no large percentage of the community will have an opportunity to participate *directly* in community decisions, except in very small towns and villages, the extremely minimal involvement found in the Syracuse study raises serious questions about the community's participation in the community development process. It suggests that extensive involvement of the citizens may be a value assumption without basis in reality. It certainly indicates that establishment and maintenance of a wide base of community participation is not easily achieved, if at all possible. Community development organizations need to strive for greater inclusiveness either through direct membership and participation or through indirect involvement. Additional research is needed to establish realistic dimensions to the concept "broad participation." Until these steps are taken, only a part of the community—and perhaps a very small part—will be making decisions we refer to as "community decisions," which affect the entire community.

Nonparticipants may not be involved because they feel excluded or because they are, in fact, excluded from the community decision-making process. Others may be apathetic. Noninvolvement seems to emerge as a typical pattern, encouraged by size of the community. The largest number of nonparticipants, however, probably remain inactive because they have never been asked to become active. They have never had an opportunity to become involved. Minority and low-income groups, particularly, have been isolated from effective participation in the community development process.

One reaction to this situation is the Office of Economic Opportunity's now famous dictum that defines a community action program as one "which is developed, conducted, and administered with the *maximum feasible participation of res-*

9. Linton C. Freeman, and others, *Local Community Leadership* (Syracuse, N.Y.: University College of Syracuse University, 1960).

idents of the areas and members of the groups served."[10] A second and more general reaction to the participation patterns found in most communities is the development of indigenous movements, many of which have a strong protest-conflict orientation. These organizations have grown in response to the limited, if not total lack of, participation of the poor and other marginal groups in the community's decision-making process, the outcome of which frequently and directly affects the poor. Haggstrom, in Chapter 4, points out the dangers both to the poor and to the community generally in this lack of involvement. He emphasizes the importance of the participation of marginal groups in the acting community.

Protest-conflict organizations, theoretically at least, would never have been organized if participation in the community development process had been inclusive, if all subgroups had been involved in community decisions and actions. These organizations developed because insufficient attention was directed to one of the three value assumptions stated earlier. The purpose here is not simply to find fault with what has not been done but to point to the serious consequences growing out of this failure to involve marginal groups.

Protest-conflict groups usually organize independently of traditional community institutions. They view themselves as set apart from the community and frequently develop a "we–they" outlook. Their major approach is to attack individuals and institutions of the community external to them and to demand changes they have established as being of high priority. Silberman, in his *Crises in Black and White*, discusses The Woodlawn Organization, which was established in a Negro slum just south of the University of Chicago. He points to TWO as an example of how Negroes living in a slum can mobilize to help themselves and can create a large, broadly representative organization—representative, that is, of *their* community, the Negro slum.

Ohlin suggests several advantages to be gained by the community from the mobilization of indigenous leadership in low-

10. Title II, Part A, Section 202 (a) (3) of the *Economic Opportunity Act of 1964, As Amended.*

income areas. These advantages all pertain to carrying out more effectively the community's participation in the community development process. First, the mobilization of indigenous leadership helps to redistribute and broaden the basis of social power. Community development does, in fact, become more inclusive and low-income groups gain a voice and a stake in the decision-making. Second, there is an increase in the personal investment of members in the established social order. Even the members of a protest-conflict organization, over time, gain a personal investment in the programs and projects they have helped to develop. Third, such mobilization provides a vehicle for recruitment and training of leaders. And, finally, a more flexible fit of major social institutions to the distinctive life styles of the local community is promoted through the efforts of low-income organizations.[11]

Other writers have pointed out some of the apparent drawbacks and problems growing out of such organizational efforts, again with the emphasis on factors affecting community participation. Three particular limitations cited are: (1) the local character and the geographically limited nature of indigenous organizations; (2) the inability of such organizations to cope with or even be relevant to major institutional change; and (3) the inability, to date, to bring these organizations together so that their combined organizational strength can be focused on problems beyond the neighborhood and beyond the city level.[12]

The effects of participation in indigenous movements on the indigenous leaders, the subgroup, and the larger community as well as problems of participation centering in the relationship between the subgroup and the external community need to be considered. Initially, the development of indigenous organizations can highlight the issues that separate the subgroup from the larger community. Such articulation may widen the gap between the two and solidify a conflict situation. While this may help to develop participation and increase involvement of

11. Lloyd E. Ohlin, "Indigenous Social Movements," in *Social Welfare Institutions*, Mayer N. Zald, ed., 180–85.

12. Frank Reissman, "Self-Help Among the Poor: New Styles of Social Action," *Trans-Action*, 2 (September–October, 1965), 32–37.

people within the indigenous organization, it can also lead to discouragement and disenchantment when and if goals are not achieved. On the other hand, even in conflict a dialogue is undertaken between the subgroup and the community, and this exchange can be viewed as a step toward joint participation and action.

The indigenous leaders, particularly, have a difficult role to play. In their contacts with the larger community they may become overly involved with the community leaders and lose touch with their own organization. If this occurs, these indigenous leaders may continue to hold the image of leadership in the external community but no longer hold positions of leadership in the low-income areas. Finally, there is the danger of role reversal whereby these leaders come to represent the external community to the low-income area rather than the low-income area to the larger community. While this discussion in no way exhausts the problems of participation between subgroups and the community, it does point to some of the areas of concern.

In summary, community leadership and social participation studies point to the fact that participation is not uniformly distributed throughout the community. In fact, decision-making is frequently centered in a rather small group of citizens. As a result, there is a tendency for subgroups of the population, particularly minority and low-income groups, to be isolated from effective participation in the larger community. In many instances this isolation has led to the organization of indigenous movements, frequently with a protest-conflict orientation. These indigenous movements bring to light a number of problems of participation centering in the relationship between the indigenous organization and the larger community.

INCLUSIVE ORGANIZATION: DIRECT PARTICIPATION. Beyond the problems and implications associated with differential participation is the more basic difficulty of the limitation on direct participation. The small rural village or the geographically limited urban neighborhood can organize to involve everyone who wishes to participate in the community development process. The problems growing out of participation through representation (which will be discussed next in this chapter) do not exist. The problems of communication are greatly reduced.

The tempo of activity is likely to be quicker in the direct participation organization than in the representative organization and the interval between decision and action brief. People can meet, decide, and act without the investment of time required in an organization where members may need to obtain official reaction from the groups they represent. The principal basis for participation is the locality; the particular issues for action are those which are of concern to the locality. If the community is small enough, issues in the field of employment, education, welfare, recreation, or a variety of other fields can be tackled by the inclusive organization. This is not true of the representative organization, in which the principal basis for participation shifts from locality to interest and attention frequently narrows to social issues to the exclusion of others.

Perhaps only in the smaller communities and through the direct participation organizations can the individual play a significant role in the life of his community. Through study and discussion a high degree of consensus may be achieved, and through planning and action the direction of change can be influenced. The face-to-face organization in the small community offers participants an opportunity to be a part of the community development process. Participants can enjoy a real sense of belonging, of direction that is established internally, not externally. At a time when the movement in organizations is toward centralization and the role of the individual seems to be decreasing, these possibilities of participation in the inclusive organization take on increased importance.

There are, of course, several limitations and difficulties associated with participation in this type of organization. The most obvious is the limited size of the community where direct participation can occur. Kaufman suggests that an inclusive membership organization ceases to be effective in localities with over one thousand population and that the optimum population is below this number.[13] This restricts participation on

13. Harold F. Kaufman, "Conception of Community in an Urban World," *Journal of Social Research*, 5 (March, 1962), 81–90, published by

a face-to-face basis to small villages and towns and to urban neighborhoods that are actually subgroups or subcommunities within communities. Even in such small communities, direct participation may be difficult.

Frequently the individual lacks identification even with the small community. Locality and interests may be quite separate. In such circumstances the individual will be less motivated toward participation. If the individual feels under some pressure to belong, he may join an organization but probably will remain an inactive, nonparticipating member. This detachment is apt to occur in fringe communities where people live, but work and form personal associations elsewhere. Scaff found that commuters in a suburban town divided their interests between their place of residence and place of work. In general, the commuter participated little in community affairs.[14]

Another limitation to participating is the realization that many problems are not accessible to solution by the community itself. Many of the issues are no longer local in nature and origin, and action on them lies outside the community. The importance of the individual's participation at the local level seems to be on the decrease. The impact that the individual and the organization can make sometimes seems insignificant. What some have tended to label apathy may, in fact, be both the lack of identification with the residential community and the recognition that the small community has very limited control over either its problems or their solutions. Under these circumstances one might anticipate a decreasing amount of participation in the community development process in the small town or village.

Exception to the above generalization would occur when issues over which the local community does exercise considerable control are under discussion. The creation of a water district, establishment of a summer recreation program, flotation of a bond issue to build a new public school, and similar matters,

the Council of Social and Cultural Research, Bihar, and the Department of Anthropology, Ranchi University, Ranchi, India.

14. Alvin H. Scaff, "The Effect of Community on Participation in Community Organizations," *American Sociological Review*, 17 (April, 1952), 215–20.

although involving resources from outside the community, are essentially local decisions. In other words, although people from outside the community may need to be consulted and involved at various stages, the decision about the issue to be discussed and the direction of change are internally established. In addition, participation may occur even where much of the decision-making lies outside the community. Then, local effort may be directed simply at modifying action in line with the concerns and interests of the local community. Whatever the future trend of the direct participation organization, much of the community development literature has been focused on activity in the small village, carried on through the inclusive organization.

REPRESENTATIVE ORGANIZATION: INDIRECT PARTICIPATION. For most citizens the community is too large to be dealt with directly; the people cannot be involved face-to-face through a single organization. In addition, because the community lacks a formally organized structure, there are no clear lines of communication and authority. If the community development process is to function with broad community participation, then some means of participation through representation must be established. The two immediate steps are the identification of the important subgroups in the community and their involvement in the community development process. The subgroups include both formal and informal organizations of the community. Their involvement in the process is through their leaders or others designated to represent them. Some of the issues and dimensions of participation and the representative organization cluster around: (1) the relationship between the subgroups and the representative organization; (2) the lack of clarity around the concept of representation; and (3) the lack of involvement of marginal, frequently unorganized, groups.

The relationship between subgroups and the representative organization is frequently poorly defined, often limited and strained, and, in some cases, nonexistent. The subgroup is usually oriented to its own locality or interest. Its first loyalty, concern, and involvement is with its own group. Participation in the representative organization usually takes second place to participation in the subgroup. Part of this ranking of interest is to be expected as one examines this relationship in greater detail. We shall look briefly at five factors bearing on this relationship.

First, there is a difference in orientation between the subgroup and the representative organization. The subgroup, because it is relatively small, places high importance on social incentives. Its reason for identifying as a subgroup and its major stimulus for action may be explained in terms of a specific issue or problem. The representative organization also is motivated by social incentives, but because of its size and the representative nature of its make-up must place major importance on group consensus. There must be some general agreement as to a direction of action that meets with the approval of a majority of the participating subgroups. Therefore, while social incentives and group consensus are important to both the subgroups and the representative organization, it is the priority each attaches to one that may lead to some strain in the relationship between the subgroup and the organization.

A second, and related, factor is the inconsistencies in objectives between subgroups and the representative organization. While their general goals may be the same, the specific objectives may not be in harmony. The representative organization may place a high priority on upgrading the public schools through a building program and the addition of special services. Subgroups may support this program, but see as the first objective the firing of the school superintendent. Although both would agree on the goal of better education, how this should be brought about and what priority should be given to specific objectives and means will vary. The greater the inconsistency between the objectives of the subgroup and the representative group, the less the participation and involvement of the subgroup. At some point, if objectives become too divergent, participation on the part of the subgroup will be discontinued and the subgroup may withdraw from the representative organization.

The pace of activity, referred to earlier with respect to the inclusive organization, is the third factor to be considered here. The subgroup may become dissatisfied with the slowness of activity and the apparent lack of progress on the part of the larger organization. This discontent may lead to a loss of interest and involvement. It also may lead to action by the subgroup in matters that are being considered by the representative organization. Even if the subgroup maintains its relationship with the larger organization, there is apt to be a continuing strain in the relationship. The subgroup will always be geared to a faster tempo and look for this same pace in others. The representative organization, on the other hand, must proceed through consensus, allowing time for two-way communications between representatives and their subgroups and the representative organization.

The sequence in which relationships are established between the subgroup and representative organization may be another factor that tends to affect such relationships. Most representative organizations build from the top down, rather than from the bottom up. An organization forms and then seeks to grow through involving subgroups, each of which has some reason to join with the others. This formation is different from an organization that develops out of an association of smaller organizations. While the resultant representative organizations may appear to be the same, there is reason to believe that a stronger relationship exists between an organization and its subgroups when the subgroups have been instrumental in bringing the representative organization into existence.

Finally, we need to examine some of the reasons why subgroups establish a relationship with a representative organization. The subgroup simply may wish to keep itself in touch with new developments in the community. Establishing a relationship is also a way of exercising some degree of control over planning in the community. A feeling on the part of the subgroup that it will enhance its own prestige by being part of a cooperative planning and development program may motivate the association. For whatever reason or combination of reasons that brings the subgroup into association with the representative organization, it is important that it be identified in order to explain some of the dynamics of the relationship between the two.

The second major dimension of participation and of the representative organization to be discussed here is the lack of clarity around the concept of representation. How are representatives chosen? Are they empowered to speak for their subgroup, or do they simply facilitate two-way communication between the subgroup and the representative organization? What, in fact, constitutes representation? The community development literature frequently discusses representation without delineating the concept and its implications. We talk of "broad representation," "representative committees," and individuals who "represent a group," without specificity as to the term or the context in which it is used.

Alexander and McCann suggest two different concepts of representation. Their writing offers the clearest thinking on the subject to date.[15] The first use of the term refers to the "authorized functioning or acting by one person in behalf of another or others." This is the sociopolitical concept of representation. The second use of the term refers to the "quality of being typical or typifying a group or class." This, they suggest, is the statistical concept of representation. This latter concept actually refers to someone who is characteristic of the central tendency of a group and is, therefore, representative of that group. In practice, this concept is inoperative. First, there would be difficulty in many instances in arriving at the so-called "statistical representative." Second, even if such a representative should be identified, he could not be considered either as an accurate sample of his group or as someone who could speak or act for them.

The other concept of representation suggested by Alexander and McCann—the first—that of authorized functioning, indicates that the individual holds certain delegated authority to act in the representative organization. The range of authority is, of course, established by his subgroup. The use of the term *representation*, according to Alexander and McCann, should be restricted to this concept. The most serious misuse

15. Chauncy A. Alexander and Charles McCann, "The Concept of Representativeness in Community Organization," *Social Work*, 1 (January, 1956), 48–52.

of the term comes when we label as representatives those who are selected by people outside of a subgroup to speak for that subgroup. Committees and organizations are frequently made up of individuals selected in this way and are then referred to as representatives of various subgroups in the community. Individuals selected in this manner are in a double bind. Since they have not been delegated authority by a subgroup, they are in no way authorized representatives of that group; they speak for no one but themselves in the representative organization. Examples of this misuse of the concept of representation are found frequently in community development organizations.

The third issue of participation and the representative organization is the lack of involvement of marginal groups. As Haggstrom discusses in an earlier chapter, these groups are part of the object community but are not included in the acting community. Even where there is no resistance to the participation of marginal groups, their lack of organization prevents their involvement, or, where they have organized, their limited efforts tend to hinder their effective involvement. If these groups are to be a part of a representative organization, additional effort will be needed in helping them to organize, in assisting them to build a relationship with the acting community, and, finally, in working with them and the larger community toward becoming a part of the acting community.

In addition to the potential difficulties that may arise between any subgroup and the representative organization, other problems may present themselves here. Lacking experience in organizational work, marginal groups may resent or reject traditional organizational procedures. They may look upon the representative organization more as an enemy than as an ally. They may be unwilling to combine their own particular interests and concerns with those of the larger organization. By the same token, community developers, having less experience in working with marginal groups, may fail to pay sufficient attention to the potential difficulties mentioned here. If the value assumption of broad or inclusive participation means anything, it means that a disproportionate amount of the time and energies of the community developer must be directed toward marginal groups.

NONREPRESENTATIVE ORGANIZATION: OPEN PARTICIPATION. Perhaps the most frequently employed participation model is that of the nonrepresentative organization. Since this includes a number of quite different ways of involving citizens, several examples will be offered. Organizing efforts frequently begin with a small number of individuals who have a particular interest or concern in a specific community issue and decide to meet to discuss it; or they have been invited to come together because they have been identified as interested community leaders; or they have responded to a call for a community meeting. In each of the three situations the citizens coming together are in no way representatives of the community as the term has been defined earlier. In two of the examples, the citizens are meeting through a self-selecting process; in the instance of their responding to a specific invitation, others have selected them.

The important point here is less how they come together but what happens after these initial meetings. If an effort is made to involve all interested parties, if participation remains open to others, if broad community involvement is not only desired but sought, then the emerging participative organization will be an effective vehicle for community development undertakings. The fact that the group does not meet the strict definition of a representative organization becomes less relevant. In fact, there are certain advantages to this type of organization. A discussion of these advantages will be followed by a consideration of some of the problems and shortcomings of this form of citizen involvement.

The principal advantages in the nonrepresentative organization lie in its simplicity of structure and procedures, openness to additional participants, and ability to act quickly. Each of these advantages is relative as compared to the representative organization. Since it is not a representative organization, it does not need structure and procedure as to seeking, certifying, and involving representatives. The nonrepresentative organization can come into existence quite quickly and can continue on an *ad hoc* basis for as long as there is interest in the organization and a purpose for continuing. While simplicity of structure and procedures is not an inherent quality of nonrepresentative organizations, a better opportunity to avoid cumbersome structure and time-consuming procedures prevails here than in the representative model.

A second advantage, which is not always utilized, is the opportunity to involve additional participants. As the organization becomes engaged in specific activities, additional citizens may become interested or the special skills of some may be needed. The ability to keep the organization open-ended has importance for the continuity of the community development process and is consistent with much that has been written earlier. The need to renew organizations is a concern of all who have worked with communities. Citizens involved at the beginning may lose interest, move away, or for other reasons discontinue their involvement. At the same time others may become interested in the organization and/or may have a particular skill that the group needs. Open participation helps to renew the organization and to maintain a membership of citizens who are interested and involved.

The ability to act quickly stems from the fact that participants speak for themselves and not as representatives of others. While this pattern reduces the broad base of community participation, it does allow the organization to act quickly—especially important in those situations in which a prompt reaction to the actions or proposed actions of others is necessary. The community may just have learned that a local factory plans to relocate elsewhere or a new program will be made available if the community can respond and meet certain conditions within a short period of time. In these and similar situations the nonrepresentative organization has the ability to meet and decide quickly and, more important, to act upon the decision.

The basic concern with the nonrepresentative organization is how well the participants reflect the major views of the community, how well they serve as the community's spokesmen. Since participants are self-selected by a few for a variety of frequently irrelevant reasons, the validity of the organization and its source of authority is always open to question. As it does lack formal authority to speak for the community, its decisions will be implemented only if a sufficient number of people are convinced that the recommended action is reasonable and in their best interest. If the nonrepresentative group is too far out of touch with the community or represents too narrow a slice of the community's life it is reasonable to assume its decisions will be ignored and its proposed actions not carried out.

In an increasingly urbanized society the nonrepresentative organization is being used more and more frequently as the vehicle for citizen participation. While there are potential dangers in an organization without a constituency, lacking or limited in "grass roots" support, and responsible to no one but its own membership, these are outweighed by the advantages that such an organizational model offers. The simplicity of structure and procedure, openness to additional participants, and ability to act quickly are three of the advantages that have been discussed here.

To summarize, participation may take place through the inclusive organization (direct participation), through the representative organization (indirect participation), or through the nonrepresentative organization (open participation). Beyond the small rural village or the geographically limited urban neighborhood, participation must be of the latter types. Three of the major issues affecting participation in the representative organization are: (1) the relationship between the subgroups and the larger organization; (2) the lack of clarity around the concept of representation; and (3) the lack of involvement of marginal groups. The nonrepresentative organization has emerged as the most frequently employed participation model.

Four Components of a Participative Organization

With this background on models of community participation, we realize that what was effective at the village and neighborhood level is less relevant today in most areas, but especially so when applied to larger and more complex communities. As Ross points out, "The town hall meeting, and all its modern counterparts, is a very simple answer to the question of participation in the life of the community. Unfortunately life is no longer simple; but has in the past fifty years changed radically. The old model is no longer appropriate."[16] In an attempt to respond to these changes, three models have been presented and discussed. We now need to review the basic components of a participative organization.

The four components to be discussed here are: (1) the base and extent of participation; (2) the locality-interest orientation; (3) sponsorship; and (4) involvement of professional staff. Introductory to this discussion is the recognition that, while issues and relationships have become much more complex, people today are better informed and better prepared (through education and experience) to participate. They also have more time available to participate if they choose to use their time in this way. The extent of the community's participation in the community development process rests upon the willingness and capacity of the people to participate. Involvement, therefore, must be relevant to these considerations.

In discussing the base and extent of participation, one is aware of the numerous efforts to describe and identify the community and the attempts to make participation as broadly based, as inclusive as possible. While all community development activity takes place within a geographical context, the emphasis on community identification, found both in practice and the literature, may be less relevant today. If we begin with people in a neighborhood, a village, a county, or a region, the issues and concerns that they express and focus upon will help to identify the relevant community. Each program or project will tend to involve a somewhat different cluster, but from this shared concern will develop an amalgamation that has relevance for the people involved and for the programs and projects in which they engage.

Concern about the public schools may involve a different base (and a different cluster of groups and individuals) than concern with air pollution. The latter example would undoubtedly call for a larger geographical base from which to draw participants. The point being made here is that the base of participation in community development should be as flexible as possible and should be related to the programs and proj-

16. Ross, "Community Participation," 107.

ects undertaken. These qualities do not do away with the concept of "community" (however defined). They do suggest that rigid adherence to geographical boundaries is not only less relevant today, but actually may impede the community development process. The later discussion on locality-interest orientation will provide additional support for this position.

The extent of participation also needs to be reconsidered. One of the value assumptions discussed early in this chapter stressed the point that participation should be as inclusive as possible. While this is an important principle, we need to consider ways in which the principle can best be carried out in practice. More attention should be given marginal groups so all important subgroups have a voice in decisions. We also need to consider the level of involvement, the degree of involvement, and the duration of involvement on the part of those participating in community development organizations. It certainly is not practical (and probably not desirable) that all people participate in all decisions.

Individuals may participate extensively over relatively brief periods of time or they may maintain minimal contact over a long period. But extensive involvement by an individual over a considerable time usually is not in the best interests of the organization or of the individual. Likewise, one person serves as chairman or president of the organization while others carry out lesser duties. Rotation and the identification and training of leadership should, in theory at least, give many participants an opportunity to serve in the major positions within the organization. Others, including outside consultants, may be involved for a limited time on a specific assignment. Greater use of people on short, specific undertakings may bring into the organization people and talents that are not readily available elsewhere and would not be available to the organization on a continuing basis.

The second component to be discussed here is the locality-interest orientation of the community development organization. The basis of social participation is less locality-oriented today and more interest-oriented, and the trend seems to indicate further emphasis on common interests rather than common geography. A number of factors help to account for this trend. The mobility of people reduces their attachment to any particular community. The separation of home and work and the increasing emphasis on specialization and professionalization of occupations place added emphasis on association with people of like interest rather than with neighbors. An orientation based on locality is further reduced by the complexity of modern society and the resultant associational ties made on the basis of special interest areas such as health, youth, housing, industrial development, and many more. This issue-interest orientation also is relevant to the first component discussed, the base and extent of participation.

These factors of mobility, separation of home and work, and complexity of modern society help to account for the decrease in locality orientation. A major argument in support of an interest orientation is that more community decisions are made outside the community. Frequently, both the cause of the problem and the solution to the problem are not to be found at the local level. Organizational efforts geared more closely to common interest than to common terrain are in a better position to include participation from the county, regional, and/or state level as determined by the particular project or program. Even representatives from the national level may become participants in an undertaking. This ability to involve participation at whatever level or levels are indicated by the nature of the project is of increasing importance in community development. Such involvement may be brief and very specific but nevertheless vital to effective decision-making.

Sponsorship, the third component, is frequently overlooked in the literature, on the apparent assumption that this factor is usually clearly established in each case and is not subject to change or even modification. Sponsorship is used here to mean both the source of financial support as well as the individuals and groups responsible for bringing the organization into being. These are frequently one and the same, but this is not necessarily so. The source of funds and the interests of those who establish the organization provide the general orientation and direction that will be followed. Although financial support may be without strings and the founders' only interest may be in an active community development organization, certain limits are frequently implicit and certain desired objectives quite explicit.

In keeping with the principles and practices of community development, an organization should be sponsored by those who come together in the organization. As difficult as this may be, it is carried out by some community development programs, particularly in urban areas. In many cases where self-sponsorship is not possible, those involved in the organization contribute at least some part of the organization's support. In general, to maintain as much direction of the organization as possible by those involved in the organization, it is important that the support for the organization come from within the organization. If this is not possible, then the organization should secure as much internal support as it can and seek outside support that is both diversified and without restriction or conditions. The sponsorship of community development programs by units of government, voluntary agencies and organizations, church groups, and others is not to be ignored. Rather, these sources are recognized as the major supporters of such programs. In each instance, however, support includes the acceptance of certain conditions and a responsibility to the supporting body. These conditions and responsibilities must not conflict with the aims and objectives of the community development organization accepting such support. Sponsorship, then, becomes an important component in a participative organization.

The fourth and final component to be discussed here is professional staff. The role of the professional in the community development process is the subject of the next chapter. Here, we simply point out that people professionally prepared for work in community development are becoming more and more important in assisting groups to organize and act. The increasing complexities of modern communities and the need to link local efforts with resources and decision-making beyond the local level are only two of the reasons for engaging trained staff. The professional does not make decisions for the community, but he does suggest how to organize to make decisions. He also may suggest alternative or dysfunctional aspects of specific actions being considered. He serves as a consultant to the organization and usually can draw upon other consultants in specialized areas that may be needed in the decision-making process.

To summarize, the base of participation should not be rigidly tied to political and geographical lines. The opportunity to participate at different levels, in different ways, and over varying periods of time should be available to meet the capacities and interests of the largest audience of participants. The locality base of participation should be de-emphasized in favor of the strong interest association of most groups and individuals and the fact that participation beyond the local level frequently is essential in arriving at local decisions. Sponsorship, particularly financial support, should come from within the group. If this is not feasible, the organization should contribute to its own support and seek outside support that is both diversified and without conditions. Finally, professional staff should be engaged early in the process to assist the organization in its formation and, later, to assist in its decision-making. The complexities of modern society, the inability to take action on many issues at the local level, and the tendency toward conformity all operate to weaken community participation. New approaches to participation need to be developed and employed that are feasible and effective and that take modern society fully into account.

CHAPTER 7

The Role of the Agent
in the Community Development Process

ROBERT MORRIS

A review of the large purposes and objectives of community development activities and of the processes utilized has already revealed the complex and difficult-to-define nature of the subject. These difficulties are in no sense reduced when one turns from a general consideration of the subject to the roles and tasks of the individuals who are occupationally engaged in the process. Even though community development generally is considered to be a process, it is carried out through the intermediary activities of individuals. In turn, these individuals range from natives of the area undergoing development to temporary residents who enter the life of this area with the purpose of cooperating with the permanent residents in an effort toward change.

The term *community development worker or agent* at once introduces a succession of ambiguities in definition. It does not mean every person involved in the process, for this would include the object of change—the resident of the area to be developed, regardless of the nature of his activity. On the other hand, to restrict the term to the temporary resident who enters the life of the community as an agent of change would exclude those development workers who are recruited from among the permanent residents of the area.

It may be best to consider as community development agents all those who are occupationally engaged in the activities discussed in preceding chapters. As a further qualification, this occupational engagement constitutes their major function over a specified period of time; in other words, employment for the community development agent means employment in some full-time capacity. However, such a definition is a convenience flawed by its own limitations, for many individuals who are engaged in the activities to be discussed are, in fact, volunteers whose sources of economic support have little to do with their community activities or whose income as agents is nominal—as for Peace Corps volunteers. Nevertheless, the definition by employment is useful in distinguishing the worker from the ordinary citizen who is engaged, in the sense the ancient Greeks and Romans were engaged, in the life of their region.

The Expert Versus the Development Agent

The most troublesome aspect of the subject is whether the community development worker has some identifiable set of tasks or skills that distinguish him and separate him from other specialists—the physician, the agronomist, the public health worker, or the teacher—who happen to be working in a development area. In like fashion, how are his skills differentiated from those of the resident population? The answers are equivocal at best, for community development is relatively new and represents an emerging occupation. At the beginning, the community development worker was, in fact, a specialist who might have certain scientific skills, such as the agronomist or physician, or he might have been a more general publicist, organizer, or lobbyist who happened to be working on behalf of the developing area. With time, the attempt to develop a district, a region, or a nation became elaborated conceptually, and a close identity between agent and the inhabitants of that area developed. This identity forced the community development worker to reconsider the old issue of relationship between the giver and the receiver, the activist and the object of his action. To engage consciously and actively in a social transformation that is at once social, economic, political, and psychological—and community development involves all of these—somehow engages all who enter into the action as both givers and receivers.

The primary concern of this chapter is to direct attention to the roles, tasks, and dilemmas that confront the individuals who enter into this activity with some new vision of participatory exchange between themselves and others. The community development agent is indeed engaged in the early stages of a developing occupation or profession.

At first, the agent has only his special knowledge and sympathy for resources; since transformation of an area involves many aspects of society, he may be a builder, economist, agronomist, physician, social worker, nurse, teacher, or other specialist. When the agent's confidence as an expert is tempered by an effective respect for the perceptions, wants, and desires of persons in the developing area, then he has begun the transformation from expert into development agent. This respect is the foundation of a philosophy that considers meaningful only that change or "development" which is wanted by the residents and in which they can all become actively engaged. To the expert's previously acquired technology or skill have been added new insight, new knowledge, and new skill for the effective engagement between himself and his beneficiary, soon to become a peer or partner.

If the task and role of the community development agent are viewed in this light, the addition of new insights to his underlying skill or technique becomes his central concern. He does not interpret his function as a review of the varieties of special techniques that have evolved in a more industrialized society and that he is bringing to a less industrially developed society. These plus skills combine philosophical orientation as well as explicit content. The aims of this chapter are, therefore, to consider what it is that the community development worker adds to his underlying or primary technical skill; to consider the major types of circumstances in which these combinations of skill are applied; and, finally, to review some of the ambiguities and uncertainties that are to be encountered in an evolving occupation. Both the agent's outlook upon the world and the resources he brings to bear in the furtherance of that outlook are here our concern.

THE VALUE FOUNDATIONS FOR DEVELOPMENT TASKS. The value foundations for these emerging roles are fairly easy to identify although difficult to translate operationally. Of the first importance is the recognition that all social groupings, whether communal or societal, are in some stage of development at all times. The natural character of human association and of social organization involves change, whether slow or rapid, whether retrograde or forward-moving into untried forms. As national social change or development has come to be better understood, and as the material benefits of an industrial society (material in the sense of health and goods) have become widely desired, there has evolved a concern that all peoples have an adequate access to these material gains. However, this humane aspiration is coupled with the recognition that social change built around material improvement brings in its wake profound psychological and cultural changes, the direction and benefit of which are often uncertain and unpredictable.

The community development worker or agent is, therefore, concerned with inducing change in society but at the same time tempering that change by the wishes and pacing of the society and individuals involved. He is inevitably concerned with the responsibility he assumes in trying to bring about change, even though this change is tempered by the deepest humanity. His concern is reinforced by knowledge that national or organizational aims do not necessarily represent complete agreement among the groups or individuals who make up the society. While the development agent may take comfort from the knowledge that someone in the society has formally invited his help, he is also uneasy because the depth of support for the request is uncertain.

While there are many examples of native or indigenous residents of an area assuming the initiating role of leadership in launching a development process, the more conventional situation is one in which the development agent is introduced through some external agency, a national government or a voluntary association. Usually, although not universally, the introduction is from an agency at the next higher level of social organization. Thus, the neighborhood of a city may be the field for agents employed by bodies organized at the level of the city, the state, or the nation; an entire town may be the object of attention from a region or a nation; a region may be the focus of action from a nation or some international body, and an entire nation may be the center for the efforts of international agencies. It is the higher level of organization that provides the employment base for most community development workers.

It follows from this circumstance that the agent is usually employed by some formal instrumentality and, to this extent, takes some of his color and some of his approach from the values and purposes of the employing body. These may range from the predominantly self-help stimulating approaches of certain church organizations to the vast social and economic development efforts conducted through national governments.

The reality of employment by some organizations external to the development area is in sharp constrast to developmental concepts about the primacy of the attitudes of the ultimate recipient. The development agent is forced to mediate between the larger collective interests and the more personal community desires. This mediating role constitutes the hair shirt of the agent. Lacking objective guides for decision, his own value system must be constantly refined or he must try to frame decisions that will satisfy both sets of demands upon his judgment.

TYPES OF COMMUNITY AGENTS. If complete analysis were available, it might well turn out that types of community agents are as various as the employing organizations. However, lacking such analysis, certain major categories of community agents can be identified. It is likely that these categories are not strictly defined, since they are formed without regard to a number of variable circumstances. More likely, these categories of agent types have some close association with types of employing organizations and with certain general philosophies about community development itself. Nonetheless, the categories do serve as a useful framework for analysis.

Various descriptive terms have been applied to the role of the development agent, descriptive terms that seek to reflect the underlying philosophical thrust believed to characterize each. Thus, the widespread use of such terms as *enabler, activist, advocate, community organizer*, etc. has emerged. For each of these terms some description can be identified. However, these terms tend to describe general ways of approaching specific problems. For example, community organization is commonly defined to mean "the art or process of bringing about and maintaining a progressively more effective adjustment between social welfare resources and social welfare needs";[1] or as "a process by which a community identifies its needs or objectives, orders these needs or objectives, finds the resources to deal with these needs or objectives, takes action with respect to them, and in doing so extends and develops cooperative and collaborative attitudes and practices in the community."[2] Once we move beyond these general definitions, the functions of the staff or workers tend to be described empirically in terms of what various workers do, rather than analytically, so that a wide range of tasks and functions are listed. Thus, the persons responsible for community organization tasks are expected to act, by turn, as administrators, analysts of social problems, fund raisers for programs, legislative activists, aides to enable others to perform responsible civic tasks on their own behalf, and as "creative leaders."[3]

In like manner, community development has been defined as "the processes by which the efforts of the people themselves are united with those of governmental authorities to improve the economic, social and cultural conditions of communities, to integrate these communities into the life of the nation, and to enable them to contribute fully to national progress."[4] The staff tasks, as described, range from helping (or "enabling") people to improve their own level of living as much as possible by their own initiative, to introducing technical and other services of many kinds.

1. Arthur Dunham, cited by Meyer Schwartz in "Community Organization," in *Encyclopedia of Social Work* (New York: National Association of Social Workers, 1965), 179.

2. Murray Ross, *Community Organization: Theory, Principles and Practice*, 40, 201–21.

3. United Nations, Department of Economic and Social Affairs, *Community Development and Related Services* (New York: United Nations, 1960).

4. Arthur Dunham, "What is the Job of the Community Organization Worker?" in *Proceedings of the National Conference of Social Work* (New York: Columbia University Press, 1948), 162–72; and Violet Sieder, "The Tasks of the Community Organization Worker," in *The Curriculum Study*, Werner Boehm, ed., 4 (New York: Council on Social Work Education, 1959).

If general definitions are not yet sufficient, another approach to the subject is that of analyzing the central practical tasks that are to be performed and seeking to categorize these tasks in some coherent and logical but less general fashion. One such effort might lead to main tasks performed by community development workers, as follows: (1) the field agent; (2) the adviser or consultant; (3) the advocate; and (4) the planner. It will be borne in mind that the individuals occupying these roles or performing these tasks seek to combine some expertness with the desire to limit the application of this expertness through some measure of participation and self-motivation of the persons affected.[5]

DEEP SOCIAL CHANGE AND THE VALUE OF EXTERNAL MEANS. As he approaches his tasks, the worker is concerned with two polar considerations that are fused in his philosophy: (1) the conviction that there are needs of a population that can be satisfied by some deep social change; and (2) a belief in the value of some external means that need to be controlled and funneled into localities in order to assist individuals and communities to satisfy their new or enlarged wants.

Application of these considerations is not simple, for the definition of needs is still elusive. At the scientific level, there are certain needs that are assumed to be universal, including the need for minimum adequate diet, suitable shelter, appropriate conditions for the preservation of health and the avoidance of disease, among others. At the most elementary level this assumption is certainly true, for no individual—unless he is ill—consciously wishes for death, hunger, or lack of shelter. What is difficult to grasp firmly, however, is just what meaning can be given these terms, and at what level health, shelter, and food shall be assured.

As the analysis varies from individual, short-term wants to the social, political, and economic changes that are required to fill these wants, the concept of relative deprivation emerges: Measured by former standards, persons may have more food,

5. See also: Arthur Dunham, *Types of Jobs in Community Development* (Columbia: University of Missouri, Department of Regional and Community Affairs, 1966).

better health, and shelter; but they may also have become aware that others enjoy wider variety, better health, shelter, and education, and ampler means for the enjoyment of a more meaningful leisure. By contrast, a minimum satisfactory condition that is better when measured only by old criteria becomes outmoded and a sense of relative want and loss results.

For the most part, a development agent begins his assignment with his own vision of the good society, but he seeks to suppress it while he ascertains to the fullest extent possible the wants and desires of the people with whom he is working. Their wants or desires may be expressed at the lowest community level: a continuous water supply, a more steady flow of simple foods, primitive health services; or they may be expressed at the national level: a modern educational system, suitable for an industrial society, or the training of manpower capable of sustaining an export economy. The development agent adjusts his vision to the goals the developing area desires and helps them strive toward these goals.

However, this respect cannot remain uncolored by the agent's knowledge and experience. He cannot help but be affected by his own convictions of what programs are best for the area. For example, the local desire to increase the tourist industry, or to develop a steel mill, or to build a modern naval force may be less functional for the well-being of that society, as perceived by the agent, than a widely distributed, family-based type of agriculture or an extensive primary educational system. The tasks of the agent usually involve some open or covert dialogue between the expressed wants of a people and his own externally derived knowledge and insight, although he seeks to discipline his expression to that of a dialogue rather than a dictation.

The other side of this equation consists of the imported means, provided by external agencies, of facilities, supplies, or knowledge that can be coupled with the native talents of the population to achieve the defined goals. Here again, a wide range in the definition of needs becomes apparent. In some places and in some circumstances, it is assumed that all that is required for change is the catalytic presence of the agent in a community. His encouragement and strength will mobilize whatever forces and resources the native population has within itself to take action and to overcome what may be centuries-old apathy and resignation to the vagaries of fate. At the other extreme is the recognition that the acquisition of any of the benefits of industrial society—the reduction of poverty, the improvement of health, etc.—requires a capital investment in the form of knowledge and tools. This capital investment might be slowly and painstakingly acquired, nation by nation, or the process of acquisition can be immeasurably stepped up by a benevolent or philanthropic sharing among nations. To the extent that the agent is committed to speeding the process, to that extent he is engaged in securing and providing, from external sources, at least some of the means required for an accelerated tempo of development. These resources may be funds; they may be materials and supplies; or they may be technical knowledge.

If these major elements are considered universal for development tasks, then what can be said of the various types of roles, noted above, of the community development worker?

THE FIELD AGENT.   The term *field agent* in this usage is closely akin to the concept of the *enabler*, commonly cited in the literature, although its meaning is narrower. He is that worker who is in immediate and continuous communication with the individuals of a neighborhood, area, or region. He it is who maintains the essential link between the external world of ideas, values, and resources and the internal situation that is subject to change. He it is who is most sensitive to the pull of tradition, to the values inherent in the society, and to their revered and painful evolution over the centuries in some symbolic relationship to the environment. He it is who is sensitive to the particular character of wants and desires expressed by the individuals.

As suggested above, this agent may identify completely with society and grope for those means by which he can stimulate the people to take the steps necessary to achieve that which they desire. Or, he may filter their expressions through his perception of their situation and seek to engage in that dialogue which will lead them to undertake direct action to alter those elements of their situation which they consider to be undesirable.

The concept of the agent or enabler draws intellectual nurture from a number of directions. The agricultural agent has learned how to speak the language of people with whom he works, although it is true that he brings a very explicit knowledge that he does not deny or abandon in the face of differing wants of the people with whom he works. The anthropologist has contributed a major respect for the vitality of any culture and for the fact that each state of social organization represents the achievable balance between the capacities of the people and their environment. The ecological or balance-of-nature concept, which is so central to community development, derives much of its strength from anthropological insights into the naturally evolved forms of social organization. The field of social welfare has contributed the concept of local community organization, through which the practical aspects of social organization are introduced to enable individuals to capitalize on the benefits of cooperative group action. This concept introduces a familiarity with the varying techniques by which individuals associate in groups, sustain their inner group character, and evolve the means by which they, the group members, can communicate with others for continuity of action. Organizing techniques developed by social workers include such elements as small-group decision-making procedures; location of responsibility for follow-up action; report-back and monitoring devices; and simple organization mechanisms to translate wants into needs.

THE CONSULTANT. Another type of community development worker is less concerned with the field situation, although he may be "in the field" for varying periods of time. He is the adviser or consultant and is usually responsible to an external employer. The consultant may have traditional expertness in health, agriculture, or economic development, but if he is to function as a community development agent, he adds to his expertness the special knowledge of how to link the external operation to the locality.

The adviser may be employed by one of the ministries of a nation—the ministry of health or of housing—that is seeking to engage the resources of the nation in the aspirations of a remote rural village; or he may be the employee of an international voluntary association that is seeking to funnel the charitable impulses of a church to a poverty-ridden region of the world. In either case, the community development consultant is concerned, as much as anything else, with those modes of behavior which will link the external concern with the realities of the local social organization and with how the interests, impulses, and resources of the external organization can be linked with those of the locality.

The adviser or consultant necessarily requires some knowledge of the local culture as well as of the external culture and acts as a bridge between the two. He may rely on the eyes-and-ears function of the field agent, or he may acquire the equivalent information by periodic forays into the culture. His advice may take the form of educating the decision-makers of the external agency about the desires and circumstances of the area being developed. His sole function may be to identify the situation in the developing area in order to organize externally planned education in the area. Or he may be trying to alter the means of communication between the external and the internal culture.

THE ADVOCATE. By contrast with both field agent and consultant, the advocate is committed to the aspirations and desires of residents in the developing area. He has identified himself with their needs and wants, regardless of the extent of "mix" between his own perceptions and those of the native population. His main function is to press the views of local needs upon the external agency in order to secure a response—favorable and helpful, if possible. Certain missionary groups have functioned—sometimes unconsciously—in this fashion, as have many secular reformers. Danilo Dolci, for example, identified himself so completely with the requirements of the Sicilian village and town that he became spokesman for the culture in trying to force from the external world attention on the needs of Sicily.[6]

The advocate is less concerned with bridging than he is with attracting attention to what he considers to be a serious situation. He may be the advocate of particular ways of resolving the dilemma or of simply directing attention to the situation.

THE PLANNER.   Finally, there is the development planner, who requires a different combination of technical skills from that of the field agent, the adviser, or the advocate. The planner usually functions at the external agent level but is responsible for designing the details of any program that seeks to alter a local situation, whether that locality be defined as a neighborhood of a city, a town, a region, or a nation. True, he is concerned with procuring some sounding of local wants and needs and local attitudes. However, his main concern is to fit local needs into some kind of national or external agency plan. In this sense, the development planner is usually a combination of technician and advocate, in the sense that those local elements which he identifies as being relevant need to be ranked in relation to other demands on the nation's resources.

For example, at the national level of any developing society, the desire of a rural village population for small landholdings and for improved agricultural equipment for family farming may have to be fitted into a national developmental plan that seeks to maximize agricultural production through industrial farming or to develop an industrial economy that will necessarily involve a relocation of population from agricultural to industrial pursuits and from village to town living. Just where each neighborhood, town, and regional want and desire is fitted into the national plan becomes the task of the development

6. Danilo Dolci, an architect and engineer by training, went to Sicily in the early 1950's for a brief visit to study ancient Greek architecture. Because of the poverty he found there, he decided to settle near Palermo and launch a campaign for the economic development of Western Sicily. See Danilo Dolci, *Report from Palermo*, trans. by P. D. Cummins (New York: Orion Press, 1959).

planner. However, technically the planner is concerned with the allocation of external resources in the form of dollars, facilities, supplies, and manpower, and with the relation of these resources to some patterning of development.

Since community development literature has so long stressed self-help objectives for individuals, groups, and communities, it is necessary to ask whether there exists a task and skill built primarily around the idea of "human development" without being tied to an underlying technical skill as well. Has there yet evolved a function for specialists *only* to help others help themselves, without relating this help to a more technically evolved concept about what the modern world requires? Is it likely that a development program for, let us say, improving rural health will employ health workers to build infant care centers and separately employ persons who will *only* work with the native population to stimulate them to move in any direction they choose as a means of stimulating self-help capacities?

In answering such questions, attention must be given to two quite separate circumstances: the facts of community development employment; the slow emergence of new professional or technical skills. A review of a large number of development programs will reveal that most development agents began their employments with some specialized skill, to which they added, often intuitively, the extra talent of arousing self-help responses from the people in the developing area. This extra talent has led to the moderating influence imposed on the expert skill, so that a dialogue has ensued between agent and people, as noted above.

One may expect, over time, that a wholly new and free-standing professional or technical skill will develop that is concerned solely with freeing persons to act on the events in their lives, without being at all concerned *technically* with the content of that on which they are acting. If this does occur, it may take on the value-free character of psychoanalysis, in which the therapist seeks to free the individual from hampering constraints. However, recent research into psychotherapy has revealed the unrecognized extent to which this therapy is heavily influenced by the latent value-biased views and behavior of the therapist.[7] Similar value-laden handicaps may also emerge in the development profession, even though it seeks to dissociate itself from specific ends or goals for the group or community being developed.

It may be more fruitful to consider the present reality of development practice rather than to speculate on the nature of a future professional form. In this time-shortened view it is clear that the community agent usually (1) combines a technical skill with the development function or (2) is assigned as a development specialist to a team or to a program or project that has explicit aims and objectives. These explicit aims may be economic development through the transformation of agricultural practices in accordance with recent scientific information; or to the introduction of new industry, which requires training in new patterns of time-use as well as training in specific new work skills for the local population; or the improvement of health levels through the introduction of new perspectives and patterns of behavior in sanitation, hygiene, infant care, etc. In such circumstances, the development worker's purposes are to free the people, *but* to free them so they may better achieve the general objectives established by the development agency itself. He may moderate the tempo of action but not its main direction. If the worker's efforts result in local opposition to the development objectives (not the timing or means), conflict ensues, for which development literature provides no guidance. The worker must himself find the resolution of the conflict.

The situation of the development worker is succinctly summarized by Dunham in a recent attempt to outline types of community development jobs. He quotes an official as saying, "We look for people with social work training in community organization [persons trained in stimulating and enabling others to act for their own ends]. We find little interest from this group in general. We are therefore forced to look to other sources where people ... seem to have used a 'community development approach' in a more specialized job, such as agri-

7. See, among others, August B. Hollingshead and Fredrick C. Redlick, *Social Class and Mental Illness* (New York: John Wiley & Sons, Inc., 1958).

culture, community relations, housing, planning. We thus end up with people educated in a variety of fields. Our young 'generalists' may be recent college graduates in most any field who show an interest and feeling for community development, and they learn on the job."[8]

It is a reasonable conclusion that, for the present and in fact, the community worker does not yet have a single or "pure" function; rather, he combines some specialized technical skill, or purpose, plus a human development feeling, out of which a new combination of skills is slowly being forged.

METHODS AND EMPLOYMENT OF THE DEVELOPMENT WORKER

Without attempting to develop any manual for the practice of the agent, it is possible to outline briefly some of the main distinguishing methods or techniques used by each of the above types of workers. It must be admitted that these functions are not entirely exclusive and that any one individual is likely to perform differing functions at different times or will have long-term responsibility for several kinds of functioning, although operations are limited to one kind at any particular period of time.

The field agent usually brings expert knowledge in some specialized field of activity. But to this is added the distinguishing characteristic of the community development field agent, that heightened self-awareness of himself as a catalyst in which his energies are used not exclusively for teaching nor for organization, but primarily to engage the interest and energy of the persons toward whom the effort is directed, so that they can organize their own energies in some meaningful fashion.

In this respect, the field agent is not an agent of change in the direct sense of dictation, creation, or construction. Rather, he constitutes a window on a different world, a portable window brought to developing groups that permits them to see a different way of living, and he then leaves to them the choice of action to achieve this different world and their rate of progress toward it.

This role entails for the agent a self-conscious development

8. See Dunham, *Types of Jobs in Community Development*, 18–19.

of behavior in which the reactions of others becomes as important as one's own acts, and these reactions are evaluated on a scale of self-actualization for others rather than on a scale of the agent's accomplishments. This behavior is difficult to pin down semantically, but it is unmistakable when observed. It involves less a didactically communicated set of techniques and more a style of life that may be acquired from observation.

A second set of methods bears more clearly the nature of technique. These methods deal with the elements of human self-organization. Here, the development agent is concerned with the ways in which individuals and family units form themselves into more formal types of social organization in order to gain the benefits of pooled energy and talent. The stress is upon varying means of establishing communication between individuals and disparate groups in a community and on the techniques by which obstructions to communication can be overcome.

Once communication and exchange have been established, it becomes necessary to identify those more formal modes of social organization which are essential if cooperative effort is to be sustained over any period of time without exclusive reliance upon the attractions of blood and family. Each society has its formal organizations that range from religious groupings, through friendship and kinship associations for protection, to organization for political decisions, etc.

What the agent introduces is the mechanism, or mechanisms, for resolving internal conflict and for arriving at group decisions that do not rely upon the hierarchy of the family or the inherited patterns of kin relationship. He introduces, when necessary, the concept that differing opinions can be valuable and that means must be found to reconcile differences in the interest of a general and useful synthesis. This concept is followed by more formal allocation of responsibility, in which the able individuals are assigned the opportunity for carrying out more or less specified tasks and can be held accountable for the results of their actions.

To these mechanisms is added the technique by which progress is evaluated and decisions made about the suitability of an earlier course of action or its replacement by a better. These techniques may be some adaptation of the town meeting, or of the committee, or of the staff and line organization of bureaucracies; or they may be adaptations of the formal organizations already developed by the society itself, but they are now infused with tasks that are essential in a changing and more urbanized or industrialized order: goal change, goal identification, responsibility for continuity, and accountability.

A third category of technique has to do with the relationships that must be forged between the community being developed and the external environment. Much has been said and written about the interlocking chain that flows from individuals in association at the family level, through their neighboring forms of organization, into successively more remote and more complex levels of human organization. Homans[9] has identified the internal satisfactions that must be met for the members constituting a given entity or group and the tasks that group must then perform in response to the demands of its external environment. Warren[10] and others, in turn, have outlined the varieties of linkage and association that bind groups together in horizontal relationship to each other in a given area and, in turn, the relationships that link these horizontal structures to the external world of greater political or economic complexity in the region or the nation.

The development of more suitable linkages between the given community and its external environment has become a specialty of its own. In historic evolution, some bonds of association have inevitably been forged, certainly, in societies that are more complex than the neighborhood or village. These bonds may have been political obligation, conquest, or trade. These fundamental linkages between the neighborhood and its external environment are now supplemented by linkages designed to draw the several levels into a common enterprise.

From the viewpoint of the area being developed, it is necessary to acquire both the means and the channels for presenting local views about wants and desires and for presenting them in terms that are understandable by quite alien and external

9. George Homans, *The Human Group* (New York: Harcourt, Brace & World, Inc., 1950).
10. Roland Warren, *The Community in America.*

groups functioning in more complex political and social systems. The presentation of views, of pleas, demands, or wants, and of proposals designed to fit the local desires is a major necessity. But these presentations inevitably involve two-way communication, and those who live in the external world must also find means for reaching into the developing area and learning to understand its requirements, its desires, its tempo. For the advocate or the field agent, this level of technique may require the most forceful presentation of neighborhood or local needs. For the consultant or planner, it demands receptivity to smaller-scale ideas and wants and the devising of means for fitting such desires into a national plan. While this fitting together may be a special technique of the planner for development, the opening of contact and communication—the "knowing how to talk to each other" and "how to listen to each other"—are of the essence for all community agents.

Another group of methods deals with the techniques necessary for the execution of plans. At the simplest level, for instance in the field of public health, the expert understands that water supply and sewage disposal need to be contained. There are well-known techniques for achieving this control in varying conditions of complexity and primitiveness. However, the development worker adds to this special knowledge some understanding of how to motivate villagers to develop their own irrigation channels, or their own wells; how the dissemination of new infant-rearing practices will best be achieved, etc.

An additional set of techniques useful for the development worker deals with the means for introducing special external resources into a locality. This is less a matter of procurement—although the sponsoring organization for change must assure that adequate resources are procured—than it is a matter of how new funds, new machinery, new expert personnel are brought into the community. These resources should enter in such a way as to maximize the self-learning and self-help capacity of the population rather than to impose a formalized learning on a reluctant population. One method may continue the established hierarchy of authority in the locality, while another may replace an old with a new set of elite leaders, and a third method will produce a wide dispersion of authority.

THE EMPLOYMENT OF THE DEVELOPMENT WORKER.   As has already been indicated, the development worker is either employed by some external organization or, if he has been an especially innovating and powerful leader, has developed his own organization. The type of employer significantly influences the goals of the development worker and his methods of working. A few types can be identified.

Perhaps most common is the development agent who is employed by a national agency, a government, or a national voluntary association, but he is assigned to the development area with certain duties. This worker is likely to be the field agent; his assigned task is to relate national aims to local circumstances and expectations, the latter needing to be explored and defined by him.

The national task may be to stimulate a form of local self-help, in the absence of sufficient national resources. In this circumstance, the development worker is concerned not only with the identification of local wants and desires, but he needs to ascertain the extent to which these aspirations are free to fall outside of any national framework of development. Where there is maximum freedom from the constraints of a national plan, there is maximum opportunity for varieties of local development. However, where major national objectives have been closely defined, the development worker is likely to be constrained by the need to fit the local aspirations somehow into this national frame if he is to continue in his appointment or if he is to secure the necessary support for his task.

The field agent's success depends heavily on the extent to which he can tap locally controlled resources. Where national objectives are most general, where national resources are least relied on, the agent has maximum freedom to stimulate local development in whatever direction the community seeks. However, if national resources are committed extensively, and if national goals have been outlined with clarity, then the agent is engaged both in persuading the developing area of the importance of these national goals and of finding a connecting link between their aspirations and the national aims.

Since most political systems are sufficiently open to require that national plans evolve with some reference to local requirements, to that extent it may be assumed that the national plan already reflects some local aspirations. In this circumstance, the agent's activities include feeding back the results of the first planning and making corrections or adaptations as changed circumstance and experience require.

A second situation is that of the development worker who is employed nationally by a national program for development. He may be fully engaged on the national level, with some field forays of his own. More often he is a program administrator to whom field agents are responsible. While such a worker is necessarily concerned with many of the foregoing considerations, his main purpose is to view local resources, desires, assets, and especially, human behavior as either resources or obstacles in national development. Depending upon the degree of elaboration in the national plan, this agent's role may be that of developing local support for the national aim, often in the guise of local education. However, this aim need not always be constrictive; its function may be to direct national activities that are designed to stimulate some—almost any—kind of local action that falls only within the most loosely defined set of national aims.

Sometimes, and more rarely, the agent is employed by a national program to transfer local needs and desires effectively into the national plan. Since this means tempering and altering the national effort, it requires that the development plan itself be an organically growing one, growing out of daily experience rather than relying on a blueprint. Since it is also difficult to manage resource allocation so flexibly, it is not often encountered.

There are situations in which locally defined groups have employed their own agents. Much of the time this employment comes about, not so much through employment in the market sense of the term, as through the individual's engaging himself with the local community to the exclusion of external organizations and becoming a part of the community.[11] In this in-

11. Advocate city planners have emerged in some cities in the United States. They are employed by neighborhood groups directly, usually at a reduced fee, and develop locally based plans as a counter-weight to metropolitan, regional, or national plans that are locally approved. In

stance, the development agent's main role may be that of the catalyst, previously described. More often it also involves the technical introduction of the locality's needs through an upward ladder of decision-making into the national resource system, which the local group requires. The agent may concentrate upon local self-help, in which case the scope and tempo of development will be greatly influenced by his skills but even more significantly by the scale of local resources. Where there is some desire to tap into a national or external reservoir of resources, the agent will be judged as much as anything by his capacity to help the local group acquire external resources. For this purpose, the organization of effective local expression is important, but no less so is knowledge about external resources and the pathways or channels through which the local group can acquire them.

Finally, there is the agent employed by an international association, either voluntary or governmental. The governmental group may be multinational or binational in character. Many of the elements discussed above will prevail, but the role of the worker differs in some significant respects. If the external sponsorship is multinational, then the agent is freed from the risk of subordinating his efforts to the special interests of any single external cultural agent. On the other hand, in these circumstances he may be dealing with conflicting views and values that will slow the tempo of change and acquisition of support as these differences are reconciled. Also, the resources for the project are likely to be more remote and the time for their procurement delayed. In similar fashion, the fluctuations of international relations introduce an element not only of distance but of instability to the local development activity.

The Conflicts and Contradictions Confronting the Agent

The task of the community development agent is complex not only because of the emergent character of this profession and the complexity of social organization, but more so because

---

such cases, the local group employs technical skill and establishes general aims only. Examples are found in New York City, Cambridge, Massachusetts, and Philadelphia.

of the varieties of apparently inevitable contradictions in value he confronts. At this stage of development it is not possible to produce any absolute guides for the individual worker to choose among these contradictions. It is possible only to identify major types of contradictions, so the agent is conscious of the choices he must make.

Perhaps the most fundamental difficulty has to do with the balance between social change and cultural preservation. Nearly all efforts to improve health or economic conditions in a given area involve some adoption of or adaptation to an industrial base. However, the introduction of industrial forms into agricultural societies produces alterations in family structure, the patterns of male and female activity, and the socialization of youth—changes that are by now widely recognized. Can poverty be really altered by changing the habits of agriculture, or do new agricultural equipment, fertilizer, and methods of marketing need to be introduced? If the latter, then the economic base and the social forms of organization need also to be altered.

It is sometimes, but not always, possible to foresee the changes that will take place in family structure, but, in the broadest terms, the greater the degree of industrialization, the greater will be the changes in family relationships and in the patterning of functions assigned to individuals. Industrialization alters the role of women, the status of the husband and father, the obligations of children, patterns of marriage, the size of household, to name only a few. In rapidly industrializing areas, these changes may appear in a very few years, even though few of them are anticipated by residents.

Related to these changes is concern about the extent to which new knowledge should be directly introduced by the development worker. Workers need to recognize that most changes desired by any group are likely to be determined by their experiences and perceptions and that where these experiences have been limited to the immediate environment, their expectations may be modest and limited in comparison to the objectives the agent knows to be possible. To what extent should the needs-and-expectations horizon of the developing area be enlarged through the catalytic or educational efforts of the development agent? If he introduces his own set of standards, the community's aspirations may far exceed local capacities; conversely, failure to introduce any new standard of comparison may result in a too limited or inappropriate change or goals.

Related, in turn, is the matter of tempo. The time sense in an agricultural society tends to be slower, the tempo geared to the seasons, whereas time sense and tempo in the underprivileged area of a large city is likely to be rapid and more erratic. If a nation seeks to industrialize and to capitalize on certain mineral resources, for example, too slow a tempo may mean that the nation or the community at no time is capable of satisfying its desires because it is unable to correlate its development with that going on elsewhere in the world. With the increasing tempo of technological development in the industrialized areas, it has become evident that the gap between have and have-not nations is widening, despite efforts to spread new methodologies and technologies more widely. Some of the difficulty may lie in the differing nature of the time sense in the highly advanced and in the less developed nations.

These and similar ambiguities for the development worker are usually moderated through two sets of quite practical decisions each agent needs to make. The first is the extent and scope of his own educational and image-building activity. How active will the agent be in trying to preserve or to alter the culture in which he is working? Whether his activity falls within the general rubric of education or of example, the effect is the same. The more active the worker, the more responsible he becomes for introducing some type of movement; the more passive, the less likely is his role to be perceived or understood.

Of equal and practical significance is the matter of resource allocation. Is the development task to be done entirely through self-help mechanisms or through the introduction of external resources? If reliance is placed upon self-help, then both the scope and tempo of action are influenced not so much by the skill of the agent (although this is important) but upon the real resources of the facilities, supplies, and skills that are available in the developing area. If the major change is desired in agronomy, are there available in the self-help area sufficient advanced farmers? If the change is desired in landholding patterns, does there exist within the developing area the political power to bring about the change? If the aim is an improvement in health status for children, are there physicians or health aides already trained? If not, are there trainers available within the developing areas?

On the other hand, if the development is to rely upon the input of external resources, then the local plan must somehow be coupled or articulated with the values, points of view, and plans of the external agent. Where the plan is the instrumentality of government in a nation, it can be presumed that priorities are fixed in a more or less crude fashion by the wishes of the population, including those of the developing area. But whether this congruence is great or small, the access to external resources is inevitably influenced by these external values and not solely by the wishes and wants of the developing people. A commitment to national aims, with concomitant access to larger external resources, inevitably requires some reduction in sensitivity to local wants and some reduction in the range of variety possible in local planning.

This preoccupation with external resources is not simply a matter of funds nor always of supplies. Perhaps the most significant of factors is the supply of skilled manpower for the execution of any changing task. An industrialized or economically developed society relies upon a vast increase in specialized manpower and upon educational facilities to produce a continuing flow of skilled manpower for varying tasks. This manpower is in short supply everywhere in the world and its application is rationed with great care. Such resources are not available indiscriminately at the demand and command of local groups. The inevitable result is that the development agent must constantly choose between the desire for infinite diversity of programs for local development groups and the strictures that always limited resources impose.

A CONCLUDING NOTE

It seems appropriate to end this book on a note of uncertainty, not from a sense of shortcoming and failure but with a clear recognition that community development has not fully emerged as a professional process. Recognition of this status is a challenge, not an admission of defeat. If community development is to become fully recognized as a process and community developers as professional practitioners some of the major implications and dilemmas presented in these chapters must be understood and resolved. Here we shall examine briefly: the political implications of the process; the local thrust of community development at a time when more community decisions are made outside the community; the potential bind that frequently places the community developer between employer and the community he is trying to serve; the problem of process continuity; and, finally, the need for greater emphasis on professional education for the workers in community development.

First, we need to consider some of the political implications of the process. Haggstrom discusses the inclusion of marginal groups in community decision-making and the new patterns of involvement and power such inclusion would produce. The various efforts to involve the poor in OEO programs and the numerous clashes between these organizations and city officials are examples of the political implications of the process.[1] Since the ideology of community development supports the broad participation of citizens in the process, new and increased involvement should be viewed as desirable. Such increased participation, however, may very well challenge and change the existing institutions of the community. It is quite reasonable to assume that different decisions would be made in the community by different clusters of decision-makers.

1. See Peter Marris and Martin Rein, *Dilemmas of Social Reform: Poverty and Community Action in the United States.* See also Daniel P. Moynihan, *Maximum Feasible Misunderstanding* (New York: The Free Press, 1969).

195

While we speak loftily of participatory democracy, those presently exercising power begin to ask nervously who else wants to become involved, why, and what changes will this larger participation produce. There is acceptance of the principle, but concern with its implementation. If the process really works, those now exercising any measure of authority will have to learn to share that authority. Much of the basic unrest in the United States today, beyond race and poverty, may be traced to the stress created when those without a voice begin the painful process of becoming involved.

Another political implication is the possible creation of a social-political process outside, but parallel to, the established political structure. If neighborhoods organize and band together on city-wide issues they, in effect, create a parallel structure to city government. At times, the emerging organization may be supportive and functional to the regular political structure, but at times the two may be at odds. Voter registration efforts, nonpartisan coalitions, and issue-based citizen groups are examples of such organizations. The fact that such efforts in the past have elected mayors, defeated congressmen, and helped pass city and state propositions attests to their political importance and indicates the political implications of such a process.

A second matter for consideration is the strong local thrust to community development mentioned by several of the authors. The "great change," as discussed by Warren, indicates that an increasing amount of the resources needed by the community and an increasing number of the decisions affecting the community come from outside.[2] Does this mean that community development will become less relevant as more decisions are made beyond the community? Not necessarily, but it does call for increased attention to the linkage of the community to the resources and power lying outside the community as a central concern of the community developer. It also suggests the importance of working out ways in which local initiative and effort can develop within a larger context and how a regional, state, or national program can remain flexible

2. Roland L. Warren, *The Community in America*, Chap. 3.

and sensitive to local interests and concerns. Lloyd Ohlin's concept of the "flexible fit" of outside programs and plans to the life style of the community is an important notion that suggests this better linkage.[3]

Another aspect of this same consideration is whether community development functions effectively beyond the local level. Although there are national development programs in a number of emerging nations, many of these can be viewed as either "top-down" directed activities with little or no room for local initiative or national programs only, in the sense that a simple national administrative framework is created in which individual and somewhat unrelated community efforts take place. While both of these are gross simplifications, they bring us back to the concern with the local emphasis of community development. Most of the experience in the United States has been on a neighborhood or small-town basis. Examples of successful metropolitan or area community development efforts are limited.

Haggstrom's reference to authentic community development raises serious questions about much of the activity that is carried out in communities today under the banner of community development. A careful review of existing programs would reveal all too frequently that important subgroups of the community are not involved and may, in fact, be excluded from the community decision-making and action process. Partisan programs may be emphasized as though they are of benefit to all. National or state objectives may be sold at the local level or, worse, disguised as locally initiated goals.

Morris adds a further dimension to this problem by pointing out that a community developer with a professional understanding of the process may find himself caught between his employer's imposed plan or program and the concerns and needs of the community he is trying to serve. Haggstrom feels there is not a large number of career opportunities for those who wish to practice authentic community development. He points out that many persons called community developers are

3. Lloyd E. Ohlin, "Indigenous Social Movements," in *Social Welfare Institutions*, Mayer N. Zald, ed., 180–85.

actually promoting and rationalizing the already formulated policies of their employers.

Sutton makes a disturbing observation in Chapter 3 when he describes the community development process, particularly the idea of continuation, and then notes how infrequently this continuity of process is achieved! The dilemma consists of knowing what makes up the process and how it should work, but being unable to make it function, in many instances. Sutton suggests both some of the reasons for this dilemma as well as practical methods for improving practice to provide continuity of process. The need for further study, particularly the evolvement of a practice theory based on empirical research, is not only necessary, but it is crucial if we hope to fashion a process that continues over time.

Establishment of continuity raises serious questions about the involvement of people in any great numbers and over any extended period of time. Ross suggests that the New England town meeting model is not workable today and that other models of participation need to be considered.[4] The Biddles note a slump in interest and involvement that plagues most community development efforts at some stage of the process.[5] The maintenance and the renewal of such organizations is a concern voiced by many community developers. Alternatives to the present limited range of organizational styles and ways of involving people need to be explored.

Professional education for community development has been referred to only briefly in this book, yet much of the future of community development rests here. The social science building blocks of this emerging profession need to be more clearly identified; there needs to be more specificity in terms of what the community developer should know and be prepared to do; there is need to articulate an emerging theory of practice; there is also a need to prepare many more people for careers in community development. Fulfillment of these needs requires a commitment on the part of colleges and universities to offer

4. Murray G. Ross, "Community Participation," *International Review of Community Development*, 5 (1960), 107–19.

5. William W. Biddle and Loureide J. Biddle, *The Community Development Process: The Rediscovery of Local Initiative*, 104–7.

professional education in community development and a commitment on the part of government to support training in this field. There can be no free-standing profession of community development without additional effort on the part of those concerned with this field of practice and with its national and international impacts.

These are certainly not all of the issues and dilemmas facing community development, nor have they been explored in any great depth. Cited here are only some of those mentioned by one or more of the authors; they are simply indicative of the range of concerns that face workers in the field. Perhaps it is best to end this book with the same words Willis Sutton used to end his chapter: "While our knowledge and theory do not yet meet the challenge, such a social achievement [the more rapid enlargement of the common good] is not an idle dream. Without knowing exactly how, we have occasionally, for a little while, fashioned the social instruments adequate to the task." Our purpose, then, is to begin to identify more clearly and to employ these social instruments in working with community people in carrying out their plans and hopes for a better community.

CONTRIBUTORS

WARREN C. HAGGSTROM, PH.D., Associate Professor, School of Social Welfare, University of California at Los Angeles.

ROBERT MORRIS, D.S.W., Professor of Social Planning, The Florence Heller Graduate School for Advanced Studies in Social Welfare, Brandeis University.

IRWIN T. SANDERS, PH.D., Professor and Chairman, Department of Sociology and Anthropology, Boston University.

DANIEL J. SCHLER, PH.D., Director of Community Services Department, University of Colorado.

WILLIS A. SUTTON, JR., PH.D., Professor, Department of Sociology, University of Kentucky.

ROLAND L. WARREN, PH.D., Professor of Community Theory, The Florence Heller Graduate School for Advanced Studies in Social Welfare, Brandeis University.

LEE J. CARY received his B.N.S. and B.S. degrees from College of the Holy Cross in Worcester, Massachusetts; his M.S.S. from the University of Buffalo in New York; and his Ph.D. from Syracuse University. He is presently Professor and Chairman of the Department of Regional and Community Affairs at the University of Missouri-Columbia.

BIBLIOGRAPHY: A SELECTED LIST

Abrahamson, Julia, *A Neighborhood Finds Itself*. New York: Harper & Brothers, 1959.

Abueva, José V., *Focus on the Barrio*. Manila: Institute of Public Administration, University of the Philippines, 1959.

Alexander, Chauncey A., and Charles McCann, "The Concept of Representativeness in Community Organization." *Social Work*, I (January, 1956), 48–52.

Alinsky, Saul D., *Reveille for Radicals*. New York: Vintage Books, 1969.

Anderson, Nels, *The Urban Community: A World Perspective*. New York: Holt, Rinehart and Winston, Inc., 1959.

Approaches to Community Development, Phillips Ruopp, ed. The Hague: W. Van Hoeve, Ltd., 1953.

Arensberg, Conrad M., and Arthur H. Niehoff, *Introducing Social Change*. Chicago: Aldine Publishing Company, 1964.

Arnstein, Sherry R., "A Ladder of Citizen Participation." *Journal of the American Institute of Planners*, 35, No. 4 (July, 1969), 216–24.

Batten, T. R., *Communities and Their Development*. London: Oxford University Press, 1957.

————, *Training for Community Development*. London: Oxford University Press, 1962.

————, *The Human Factor in Community Work*. London: Oxford University Press, 1965.

————, *The Non-Directive Approach in Group and Community Work*. London: Oxford University Press, 1967.

Bennett, Austin E., *Reflections on Community Development Education*. Orono, Maine: PICS, University of Maine, 1969.

Beran, D. L., *People in Action: A Handbook for Community Developers*. Columbia, Missouri: The Author, 1968.

Biddle, William W., and Loureide J. Biddle, *Encouraging Community Development: A Training Guide for Local Workers*. New York: Holt, Rinehart and Winston, Inc., 1968.

————, *The Community Development Process: The Rediscovery of Local Initiative*. New York: Holt, Rinehart and Winston, Inc., 1965.

Bloomberg, Warner, Jr., "Community Organization," in *Social Prob-*

lems: A Modern Approach, Howard S. Becker, ed. New York: John Wiley & Sons, Inc., 1966.

Brokensha, David, and Peter Hodge, *Community Development: An Interpretation.* San Francisco: Chandler Publishing Company, 1969.

Bruyn, Severyn T., *Communities in Action: Patterns and Process.* New Haven: College & University Press, 1963.

Cary, Lee J., "Resident Participation: Dominant Theme in the War on Poverty and Model Cities Program." *Community Development Journal,* 5, No. 2 (April, 1970), 73–78.

Centrally Planned Change: Prospects and Concepts, Robert Morris, ed. New York: National Association of Social Workers, 1964.

The Church and Community Organization, John R. Fry, ed., New York: National Council of Churches, 1965.

Citizen Participation in Urban Development, Vol. I, *Concepts and Issues,* Hans B. C. Spiegel, ed. Washington, D. C.: NTL Institute for Applied Behavioral Science, 1968.

Citizen Participation in Urban Development, Vol. II, *Cases and Programs,* Hans B. C. Spiegel, ed. Washington, D. C.: NTL Institute for Applied Behavioral Science, 1969.

Clark, Kenneth, and Jeannette Hopkins, *A Relevant War Against Poverty: A Study of Community Action Programs and Observable Social Change.* New York: Harper Torchbooks, 1970.

Clinard, Marshall B., "Evaluation and Research in Urban Community Development." *International Review of Community Development,* 12 (1963), 187–98.

———, *Slums and Community Development: Experiments in Self Help.* New York: The Free Press, 1966.

Coleman, James S., *Community Conflict.* Glencoe, Ill.: The Free Press, 1957.

Community Development. Study Conference on Community Development, Aylesbury, England, 1957. London: Her Majesty's Stationery Office, 1958, reprinted, 1963.

Community Structure and Analysis, Marvin B. Sussman, ed. New York: Thomas Y. Crowell Company, 1959.

Cousins, William J., "Community Development—Some Notes on the Why and the How." *Community Development Review,* 7 (1957), 24–30.

Development Administration, Irving Swerdlow, ed. Syracuse: Syracuse University Press, 1963.

Dube, S. C., *India's Changing Villages: Human Factors in Community Development.* Ithaca: Cornell University Press, 1958.

Dunham, Arthur, "The Outlook for Community Development—An

International Symposium." *International Review of Community Development,* 5 (1960), 33–55.

Du Sautoy, Peter, *Community Development in Ghana.* London: Oxford University Press, 1958.

———, *The Organization of a Community Development Programme.* London: Oxford University Press, 1962.

Dynamics of Development: An International Development Reader, Gove Hambidge, ed. New York: Frederick A. Praeger, Inc., 1964.

Eaton, Joseph W., "Community Development Ideologies." *International Review of Community Development,* 11 (1963), 37–50.

Forces in Community Development, Dorothy Mial and H. Curtis Mial, eds. Washington, D. C.: NTL Institute for Applied Behavioral Science, 1961.

Foster, Ellery, "Planning for Community Development Through Its People." *Human Organization,* 12 (Summer, 1953), 5–9.

Foster, George M., *Traditional Cultures and the Impact of Technological Change.* New York: Harper & Row, Publishers, 1962.

Friedman, Frederick G., *The Hoe and the Book: An Italian Experiment in Community Development.* Ithaca: Cornell University Press, 1960.

Galbraith, John Kenneth, *Economic Development.* Cambridge, Mass.: Harvard University Press, 1964.

Goodenough, Ward H., *Cooperation in Change.* New York: Russell Sage Foundation, 1963.

Gove, Walter, and Herbert Costner, "Organizing the Poor: An Evaluation of a Strategy." *Social Science Quarterly,* 50, No. 3 (December, 1969), 643–56.

Green, James W., "Community Development as Economic Development: The Role of Value Orientations." *Community Development Review,* 5 (September, 1960), 8–27.

Greer, Scott, "Political Participation in Urban Areas." *Community Leadership and Decision-Making: Proceedings of the Third Annual Urban Policy Conference.* Iowa City: Institute of Public Affairs, The University of Iowa, 1966.

Grosser, Charles F., "Community Development Programs Serving the Urban Poor." *Social Work,* 10 (July, 1965), 15–21.

Haggstrom, Warren, "The Power of the Poor," in *Poverty in America,* Louis A. Ferman, Joyce L. Kornbluh, and Alan Haber, eds. Ann Arbor: The University of Michigan Press, 1965.

Harper, Ernest B., and Arthur Dunham, *Community Organization in Action.* New York: Association Press, 1959.

Hayes, Samuel P., Jr., *Measuring the Results of Development Projects.* Paris: UNESCO, 1959.

Hendry, Charles E., "Community Development." *Encyclopedia of Social Work*, 15th ed. New York: National Association of Social Workers, 1965.

Hill, Ellen B., "Reflections on Assistance to Developing Countries." *International Review of Community Development*, 15–16 (1966), 43–54.

Hoffer, Charles R., "Social Action in Community Development." *Rural Sociology*, 23 (March, 1958), 43–51.

Hoiberg, Otto, *Exploring the Small Community*. Lincoln: University of Nebraska Press, 1955.

Horowitz, Irving, *The Three Worlds of Development*. New York: Oxford University Press, 1966.

Hunter, David R., "Politics and Citizen Participation," in *The Slums: Challenge and Response*. New York: The Free Press, 1965.

Hunter, Floyd, *Community Power Structure*. Chapel Hill: The University of North Carolina Press, 1953.

Hyman, Herbert H., Gene U. Levine, and Charles R. Wright, *Inducing Social Change in Developing Communities*. UN: United Nations Research Institute for Social Development, 1967.

Janes, Robert W., "Measures of Effective Community Development: An Appraisal of Community Action as a Social Movement." *International Review of Community Development*, 8 (1961), 5–13.

Jones, Garth N., "Strategies and Tactics of Planned Organizational Change: Case Examples in the Modernization Process of Traditional Societies." *Human Organization*, 24 (Fall, 1965), 192–200.

Kaufman, Harold F., "Toward an Interactional Conception of Community." *Social Forces*, 38 (October, 1959), 8–17.

————, and Lucy W. Cole, "Sociological and Social Psychological Research for Community Development." *International Review of Community Development*, 4 (1959), 193–211.

King, Clarence, *Working with People in Community Action*. New York: Association Press, 1965.

Kramer, Ralph M., *Participation of the Poor: Comparative Community Case Studies in the War on Poverty*. Englewood Cliffs, N. J.: Prentice-Hall, 1969.

Lerner, Daniel, and Wilbur Schramm, *Communication and Change in the Developing Countries*. Honolulu: East-West Center Press, 1967.

Lippitt, Ronald, Jeanne Watson, and Bruce Westley, *The Dynamics of Planned Change*. New York: Harcourt, Brace & World, Inc., 1958.

Lowry, Ritchie P., "The Myth and Reality of Grass-Roots Democracy." *International Review of Community Development*, 11 (1963), 3–15.

Lyfield, William G., and Warren H. Schmidt, "Trends in Community Development—Some Results of a Survey." *International Review of Community Development*, 4 (1959), 33–40.

McClusky, Howard Y., "A Dynamic Approach to Participation in Community Development." *Journal of the Community Development Society*, 1, No. 1 (Spring, 1970), 25–32.

McCord, William, *The Springtime of Freedom: The Evolution of Developing Societies*. New York: Oxford University Press, 1965.

Maddick, Henry, *Democracy, Decentralization and Development*. London: Asia Publishing House, 1963.

Marris, Peter, and Martin Rein, *Dilemmas of Social Reform: Poverty and Community Action in the United States*. New York: Atherton Press, 1967.

Mayer, Albert, *Pilot Project, India*. Berkeley: University of California Press, 1958.

Mezirow, Jack D., *Dynamics of Community Development*. New York: Scarecrow Press, Inc., 1963.

Mial, Curtis, and Dorothy Mial, *Our Community*. New York: New York University Press, 1960.

Miniclier, Louis M., "Community Development in the World Today—Ten Years of Progress." *Community Development Review*, 7 (June, 1962), 69–74.

Morris, Robert, "The Social Dimension of Urban and Regional Planning: An Attempt at Definition." *International Review of Community Development*, 15–16 (1966), 201–12.

Nagpaul, Hans, "Conformity and Community Development." *International Review of Community Development*, 11 (1963), 105–18.

Nair, Kusum, *Blossoms in the Dust: The Human Element in Indian Development*. New York: Frederick A. Praeger, Inc., 1962.

National Association of Social Workers, *Community Development and Community Organization: An International Workshop*. New York: National Association of Social Workers, 1961.

Neighborhood Organization for Community Action, John B. Turner, ed. New York: National Association of Social Workers, 1968.

Nelson, Lowry, Charles E. Ramsey, and Coolie Verner, *Community Structure and Change*. New York: The Macmillan Company, 1960.

Niehoff, Arthur H., *A Casebook of Social Change*. Chicago: Aldine Publishing Company, 1966.

Ogden, Jean, and Jess Ogden, *These Things We Tried.* Charlottesville: University of Virginia Extension, 1947.

Ohlin, Lloyd E., "Indigenous Social Movements," in *Social Welfare Institutions,* Mayer N. Zald, ed. New York: John Wiley & Sons, Inc., 1965, 180–85.

Our Changing Rural Society: Perspectives and Trends, James H. Copp, ed. Ames: The Iowa State University Press, 1964.

Patterns of Community Development, Richard Franklin, ed. Washington, D. C.: Public Affairs Press, 1966.

Perspectives in Developmental Change, Art Gallaher, Jr., ed. Lexington: University of Kentucky Press, 1968.

Perspectives on the American Community, Roland L. Warren, ed. Chicago: Rand McNally & Company, 1966.

The Planning of Change: Readings in the Applied Behavior Sciences, Warren G. Bennis, Kenneth D. Benne, and Robert Chin, eds. New York: Holt, Rinehart and Winston, Inc., 1961.

Polson, Robert A., "Theory and Methods of Training for Community Development." *Rural Sociology,* 23 (March, 1958), 34–42.

Popenoe, David, "Community Development and Community Planning." *Journal of the American Institute of Planners,* 33, No. 3 (July, 1967), 259–65.

Poston, Richard W., *Democracy Speaks Many Tongues.* New York: Harper & Row, Publishers, 1962.

Pye, Lucian W., "The Social and Political Implications of Community Development." *Community Development Review,* 5 (December, 1960), 11–21.

Readings in Community Organization Practice, Ralph M. Kramer, ed. Englewood Cliffs, N. J.: Prentice-Hall, 1969.

Ross, Murray G., "Community Participation." *International Review of Community Development,* 5 (1960), 107–19.

———, with B. W. Lappin, *Community Organization: Theory, Principles and Practice,* 2d ed. New York: Harper & Row, Publishers, 1967.

Rossi, Peter, and Robert A. Dentler, *The Politics of Urban Renewal.* New York: The Free Press, 1961.

Sanders, Irwin T., *The Community: Introduction to a Social System.* New York: The Ronald Press Company, 1958; 2d ed., 1966.

———, "Theories of Community Development." *Rural Sociology,* 23, No. 1 (March, 1958), 1–12.

Schneider, Kenneth R., "Reconstitution of Community." *International Review of Community Development,* 15–16 (1966), 19–42.

Selected Perspectives for Community Resource Development, Luther T. Wallace, Daryl Hobbs, and Raymond D. Vlasin, eds. Raleigh,

N. C.: Agricultural Policy Institute, School of Agriculture and Life Sciences, North Carolina State University, 1969.

Sherrard, Thomas, "Community Organization and Community Development: Similarities and Differences." *Community Development Review*, 7 (June, 1962), 11–20.

Shields, James J., Jr., *Education in Community Development: Its Function in Technical Assistance*. New York: Frederick A. Praeger, Publishers, 1967.

Shiner, Patricia, Peggy Wireman, and Lee J. Cary, *Community Development in Urban Areas: A Summary of Pertinent Journal Articles and Book Chapters*. Columbia: Department of Regional and Community Affairs, University of Missouri, 1969.

Sigel, Roberta S., "Citizen Committees—Advice vs. Consent." *Trans-Action*, 4 (May, 1967), 47–52.

Social Change: Sources, Patterns and Consequences, Amitai Etzioni, and Eva Etzioni, eds. New York: Harper & Row, Publishers, 1965.

Social Innovation in the City: New Enterprises for Community Development, Richard S. Rosenbloom and Robin Marris, eds. Cambridge, Mass.: Harvard University Press, 1969.

Sociology in Action: Case Studies in Social Problems and Directed Social Change, Arthur B. Shostak, ed. Homewood, Ill.: Dorsey Press, 1966.

Sower, Christopher, John Holland, Kenneth Tiedke, and Walter Freeman, *Community Involvement*. Glencoe, Ill.: The Free Press, 1957.

————, and Walter Freeman, "Community Involvement in Community Development Programs." *Rural Sociology*, 23 (March, 1958), 25–33.

Spicer, Edward H., *Human Problems in Technological Change*. New York: Russell Sage Foundation, 1952.

Stensland, Per, "Some Prerequisites for Community Development." *International Review of Community Development*, 6 (1960), 81–90.

Strategies of Community Organization: A Book of Readings, Fred M. Cox, John L. Erlich, Jack Rothman, and John E. Tropman, eds. Itasca, Ill.: F. E. Peacock Publishers, Inc., 1970.

Sutton, Willis A., Jr., and Jiri Kolaja, "The Concept of Community." *Rural Sociology*, 25 (June, 1960), 197–203.

————, "Elements of Community Action." *Social Forces*, 38 (1960), 325–31.

Swezey, R. Curtiss, and John J. Honigmann, "American Origins of Community Development." *International Review of Community Development*, 10 (1962), 165–76.

Tumin, Melvin M., "Some Social Requirements for Effective Community Development." *Community Development Review,* 11 (1958), 1–39.

United Nations, *Social Progress Through Community Development.* New York: United Nations, 1955.

United Nations, Bureau of Social Affairs, *International Survey of Programmes of Social Development.* New York: United Nations, 1959.

United Nations, Office for Public Administration, *Public Administration Aspects of Community Development Programmes.* New York: United Nations, 1959.

United Nations, Secretary-General, *Community Development in Urban Areas.* New York: United Nations, Department of Economic and Social Affairs, 1961.

United Nations, Division for Public Administration, *Decentralization for National and Local Development.* New York: United Nations, 1962.

United Nations, *Ad Hoc* Group of Experts on Community Development, *Community Development and National Development.* New York: United Nations, 1963.

Warren, Roland L., *The Community in America.* Chicago: Rand McNally & Company, 1963.

———, "The Good Community—What Would It Be?" *Journal of the Community Development Society,* 1, No. 1 (Spring, 1970), 14–24.

Wilkening, E. A., "Some Perspectives on Change in Rural Societies." *Rural Sociology,* 29 (March, 1964), 1–17.

Young, Frank W., and Ruth C. Young, "The Sequence and Direction of Community Growth: A Cross-Cultural Generalization." *Rural Sociology,* 27 (December, 1962), 374–86.

———, "Toward a Theory of Community Development," in *Social Problems of Development and Urbanization, VII.* United Nations Conference on the Application of Science and Technology for the Benefit of the Less Developed Areas. Washington, D. C.: Government Printing Office, 1963.

INDEX

DATE DUE

FEB 26 1975			
MAR 1 3 1975			
NOV 9 1978			
NOV 2 1 1978			
MAY 1 2 1980			
MAR 2 8 1983			
DEC 9 1984			
APR 1 7 2014			

GAYLORD

PRINTED IN U.S.A.